ENGLAND'S
BOXING
HEROES

ENGLAND'S
BOXING
HEROES

Frank McGhee

BLOOMSBURY

SPORTS EDITIONS LIMITED

Art Director   *Mary Hamlyn*
Designers   *Sandra Cowell*
                   Rob Kelland
                   Adrian Waddington
Editor   *Geraldine Christy*
Indexer   *Valerie Lewis Chandler*

First published in 1988 by Bloomsbury Publishing Limited
2 Soho Square,
London W1V 5DE

ISBN 0 7475 0273 0

Produced, edited and designed by Sports Editions Limited
3 Greenlea Park,
Prince George's Road,
London SW19 2JD

Set in 10½ point Garamond
Typeset by Typesmiths, London
Printed in Great Britain by
Purnell Book Production Limited
Member of the BPCC Group

CONTENTS

ACKNOWLEDGEMENTS

Muhammad Ali and Henry Cooper, Joe Frazier and Joe Bugner, Randolph Turpin and Sugar Ray Robinson – and most of the fighters whose names figure on the pages of this book – could not have known they were once all together on the top deck of a 143 bus travelling from Hendon Central to another north London suburb, East Finchley. A cocky, precocious fifteen-year-old school-leaver setting out on his own career in journalism did not realise it either on that early summer day just after the end of World War II.

The adolescent dreamer in the front seat, with a collar bone which still bore the strap marks of a school satchel, was me. I was wearing my first real grown-up suit from the Fifty Shilling Tailor, after a wild squandering of the family's clothing coupons in those distant days when everything was rationed except hope and ambition – and in my case a whole lot of luck. I had paid my own fourpenny bus fare on that ride to the offices of a local weekly newspaper, *The Finchley Press,* for an interview with the first of the many editors who have paid for my fares ever since … and for those hotel bills, motor cars and the occasional bout of what Peggy, my wife, with sardonic euphemism calls "Fleet Street 'Flu" – it is her name for a hangover.

That bus ride was the beginning of a journey to many distant lands, trips shared with many of those boxers and with many good colleagues who remain great friends. Among them are Ken Jones of *The Independent,* who was in on the start of this book; Hugh McIlvanney *(The Observer)* and Ian Wooldridge *(Daily Mail)*, who both grow

sportswriting awards in their greenhouses and seem to pluck them annually. There is a whole Rugby XV of them plus substitutes: Reg Gutteridge, the ITV commentator who still wields a mean wisecrack; Harry Carpenter (BBC); Colin Hart *(Sun),* Peter Moss *(Daily Mail);* Syd Hulls *(Daily Express);* Sri Sen *(The Times);* Don Saunders *(The Daily Telegraph);* Peter Batt *(Sunday Mirror);* Ron Wills *(Daily Mirror);* Patsy Collins *(Mail on Sunday)*; Brian Glanville *(Sunday Times);* Frank Butler and later Fred Burcombe *(News of The World)*; and Neil Allen *(Evening Standard)*. Some of them, sadly, are gone – big Sam Leitch of the BBC and ITV, George Whiting *(Evening Standard)* and, above all, the great Peter Wilson, who was to become a sort of journalistic older brother.

They were all in my imagination on the top deck of that 143 bus. Many of them were at some of the most significant stops on the ride that was to go round the world several times and take in seven World Cups, four Olympiads – I wriggled out of a couple because I don't much care for The Games – and more than seventy world title fights – plus more British and European championships than I care to count. They were all great companions, a lively, occasionally licentious lot worth a book of their own. I think I'll call it "Forgive us our Presspasses".

To all those sportswriters, and to my own boxing heroes, I extend my thanks for many years of enjoyment.

Frank McGhee
Weston Turville, 1988

MARQUIS OF QUEENSBERRY

INTRODUCTION

Boxing is one of the only two basic sports – running is the other. Fighting is so basic that men will always respond to its instinctive inner compulsion. It is an instinct inborn into so many. Others will always be fascinated by a desire to watch combat between the best. Yet, this is a sport that so many wish to ban. If the sport were ever outlawed it would spring up illegally underground – without the protection provided by increasingly stringent medical precautions. Yes, men do get hurt, even very occasionally killed, though no one mourns ring deaths with more genuine sadness and concern than the boxing world. But the mortality rate is significantly higher in many other so-called harmless sports, including soccer, rugby, motor racing and mountain climbing – and nobody forces a man to fight for the better living so many boxers have achieved, such as Henry Cooper, Dave Charnley, Johnny Pritchett.

Throughout my own lifetime boxing has reportedly been dying at various times, yet at the moment it is flourishing more vigorously in Britain than it has for many years. In 1987 there were more than a thousand officially licensed professional boxers and almost three hundred promotions to pay their wages.

From childhood, boxing was always a favourite sport of mine, as a spectator, not as a participant. I was, however, coached at Youth Club level by former British Lightweight Champion, Fred Webster. He scorned my attacks with, "You couldn't hit a cow on the bum with a banjo", but taught me the value of a good straight left – painfully. Whatever talent I had as a boxing boy wonder lay in gathering and storing every scrap of information available about those who really could do the business. As an infant I could name all the world champions in the then eight divisions, recite them like a litany. I can no longer do that and defy almost anyone else to do so because of the ludicrous proliferation of titles under three different and usually differing ruling authorities. Between them the World Boxing Council, the World Boxing Association and the International Boxing Federation sometimes recognise three separate world champions at each of fifteen weight divisions. It means a confusing ever-changing kaleidoscope of more than forty "champions of the world" at the same time – diminishing all but the very best. The reasons for this situation are purely commercial. Promoters and TV companies can sell a fight to gullible customers more easily if it carries a world championship label, however spurious. The one section of the boxing community who remain completely innocent are, of course, the boxers themselves.

Of all the hundreds, maybe even thousands, of sportsmen I have known, sometimes very well, over almost forty years spent mainly watching and writing about them, definitely the most decent, dignified, sportsmanlike, controlled and even occasionally noble, were the boxers. Only top golfers come close, but then someone like Nick Faldo does not have to keep his head while an opponent is trying to punch it loose from his shoulders. Footballers, regrettably, have tended to become rather greedy and self-inflated by egos and agents, and would, if they could, charge a fee for revealing kick-off times. Athletes, for all their dedication, are loners who shun head-to-head confrontation with someone who might beat them unless the big money or a gold medal is there. Too many tennis players have unspeakable on-court manners.

Boxing teaches control and sportsmanship, and builds character – something else the would-be abolitionists might reflect upon. Anyone who follows the sport regularly treats as perfectly normal the sight of two young fit men who try within a set of rules to do serious harm to one another, yet embrace with genuine affection and respect at the final bell. Those sentiments are lasting which explains why the sport is unique in the remarkable number of Ex-Boxers' Associations that flourish all over the country, meeting regularly, swapping "remember whens", staging functions, and helping colleagues who have fallen on hard times.

Joe Frazier, a great World Heavyweight Champion, once summed up a fighter's feelings about an opponent, to whom he had done – and from whom he had received – considerable damage. Remembering his three epic fights with Muhammad Ali and all the insults and ill-feeling that surrounded them, I asked whether the hatred that apparently filled those fights and fuelled both men, was genuine. He laughed and said, "Listen, when you have spilled and tasted a man's blood and smelled his sweat and made a million dollars, you don't hate him." The same Frazier completely captured all the natural dignity of the genuine fighting man when, on the morning after George Foreman had knocked him down half a dozen times in Jamaica to take his titles, he appeared for an interview and when offered a chair said, "No thanks, I think I sat down often enough last night".

I covered my first World Heavyweight Championship in America in 1956 when Floyd Patterson stopped Archie Moore in Chicago and the link that lasts right through to today was the wise teacher, trainer and manager of Patterson, Cus D'Amato, who found, and until his death was the father-figure of, Mike Tyson. The last job before I retired from the *Daily Mirror* was Barry McGuigan's wonderful World Featherweight Championship victory over Eusebio Pedroza in June 1985. I always felt that forty years at work is enough for any man. The only reason, incidentally, why Barry's story is not also in the book is his proud-to-be-Irish heritage. This book is solely about England's boxing heroes.

Some of the fighters in the book have been included because they are before-my-time legends, whose fascinating backgrounds demanded their niche – men such as Bob Fitzsimmons, Bombardier Wells, Matt Wells, Joe Bowker and "Digger" Stanley. Some were the heroes of boyhood – Teddy Baldock, Nel Tarleton, Jock McAvoy, Len Harvey, "Kid" Berg, Boon, Danahar and Crowley. Those who fought in what I still think of as recent times – anything from 1950 onwards – were men I saw and mostly knew personally, some very well. Henry Cooper, for instance, once typically freely gave up the time for which he can still charge handsomely to bring his three Lonsdale belts to my son's Junior School and hold an enthralled audience in the palm of his hand – the left hand, of course. Afterwards at a family dinner he had a Polaroid photograph taken with my then teenage daughter, who still treasures his autographed caption, "The only girl I ever belted".

The men in the book, my own choice incidentally, so you know who to blame if any of your favourites are not featured, cover the whole range of what boxing is all about. There are the ferocious one-punch hitters, like Eric "Boy" Boon; the men whose victories shook the world as Randy Turpin and Lloyd Honeyghan did; the brilliant pure boxers, Baldock and Tarleton; all-action battlers "Kid" Berg, "Kid" Lewis and Terry Downes.

They all helped to make my own writing-about-fighting life richer in every way and I hope that reading about them adds something to yours. People often ask if I miss the world of sportswriting and the answer, truthfully, is no. Sport changed a great deal in my time with increasing commercialism, professionalism, nationalism, hooliganism, drug-taking and cheating. None of that added to the enjoyment.

And, thankfully, I do not have to miss boxing. Even though two of the top promoters, Micky Duff and Frank Warren, did not always like what I wrote – any more than they like each other – both cheerfully have sent off press ringside seats for world championships they promoted in my retirement days. Don't tell either of them, but it is one sport I would still pay to watch!

BOB FITZSIMMONS
(1862 — 1917)

The most famous single punch in the whole history of boxing was thrown by a man born in the motherland of that sport: England. He was Robert James "Bob" Fitzsimmons, who was born in the Cornish village of Helston on 26 May 1862, and there will be no prizes for guessing that the punch was the left hook to the body which felled "Gentleman Jim" Corbett in the fourteenth round at Carson City, Nevada, on 17 March 1897 and made Ruby Robert Heavyweight Champion of the world. So many words have been written about that single blow that they almost obscure the fact that he threw very many more in his time.

When a man wins three world titles at different weights they immediately, automatically, and quite rightly, start cutting him his own key to The Hall of Fame. You might win a few wagers with those who know no better by asking who was the first to accomplish the feat. The favourite will almost certainly be "Homicide Hank" Armstrong of the 1930s. In fact it was, of course, the man who remains – and is likely to remain for the foreseeable future – the only English-born fighter ever to win the biggest prize in sport. England cannot really claim any other credit than providing the setting for the first smack ever suffered by what must have been a remarkably unlovely little boy baby – if the physical appearance of the man he grew up to be is any guide. The two most frequently used adjectives to describe him were "freakish" and "ugly". He was bald from an early age apart from sparse tufts of ginger hair which contributed to his other nickname, "Ruby Robert". He had a bony face with a long nose – and it is worth a small pause right there. Any man who fights for more than thirty years, starting in the bare-knuckle days, and finishes up with a nose that even resembles a nose must have more than a grasp of the rudiments of defence.

His physique was admittedly freakish, but then, looked at another way, if an expert in genetic engineering set out to create the perfect specimen to live a successful career fighting men who weighed up to 15 stone and more while he himself was never more than a heavy

middleweight (11 stone 13lbs when he beat Corbett), that specimen would look very much like Bob Fitzsimmons. From the waist down he was skinny, knock-kneed, flat footed, with the sort of legs that looked as though they would not carry a postman on a daily round. From the waist up he was a heavyweight, with ropes of muscle rippling across his back, biceps like grapefruit and CinemaScope shoulders.

He never fought in England, emigrating as a child to New Zealand, where he attracted the attention of bare-knuckle champion Jem Mace and won three amateur championships as a teenager, then turned professional in Australia. But it was not until he went to the USA in 1890 at the age of 28, when fighting careers are usually at their peak if not in decline, that his started to soar. A possibly apocryphal story at the time was that, embarrassed by the scorn his physique attracted among spectators, he used to pad the tights he wore with cotton wool to make his stilt-like legs appear muscular. Inside the ring few laughed at him – and none after January 1891 when he knocked down the original Jack Dempsey thirteen times in thirteen rounds to win the Middleweight Championship of the world. Dempsey, known as "The Nonpareil", had lost only once previously in a career of thirteen years – 68 fights.

In those days a common distance for fights was twenty rounds. Few of Ruby Robert's went beyond the first few and most of these were against heavyweights, which is not quite as unusual as it would be today because there was no officially recognised light heavyweight division until 1903. From the time he won the middleweight title the ambition of Fitzsimmons was the big one and the years he had to wait contributed to the bad blood between him and Gentleman Jim Corbett.

At one stage Corbett even retired and nominated one Peter Maher to succeed him. Fitzsimmons took less than one round to demolish the Irishman in February 1896 and it was very much "by public demand" that they finally came together in the mining town of Carson City just over one year later. A report of that fight in a publication called *The Mirror of Life* starts : "Morning broke clear and cool over Carson City. The entire population and the 5,000 visitors were awake early, crowding the streets and the so-called hotels. The crowd moved early to the amphitheatre. At the entrance everyone was searched for weapons and those at fault were turned back". The fighters were in the arena by nine, due to start punching at ten, but in fact did not get into the ring until nearly noon. It was probably just as well that the spectators had been dis-armed.

The blow-by-blow report of the fight itself confirms much of the legend surrounding it. Fitz, who only just beat the count in the sixth round, was generally outboxed and was bleeding profusely by the start of the fourteenth. Those who knew him well insist that he was not nearly as

There is an ominous, confident smile on the face of Fitzsimmons as he parries a left from Corbett.

troubled as he looked, that he was just waiting, punching throughout the fight uncharacteristically at Corbett's handsome head so that the champion's guard would create the chance that eventually inevitably arrived. Corbett was caught coming in with his hands too high by a tremendous left hook to the solar plexus. He was not unconscious, he could hear the count but the legs simply would not obey his brain and impel him to his feet.

But if you think about it, it is an insult to the intelligence to suggest, never mind believe, that Bob Fitzsimmons invented that punch. It had existed since bare-knuckle days and Fitzsimmons was simply more aware of its devastation than most. He earned his place on the pinnacle and although he did not win any medals for refusing to give Corbett a return, it was the fashion in those days to cash in on the title with theatre tours and exhibitions. Bob's next real fight was two years later when, now aged 37, the giant Jim Jeffries knocked him out in eleven rounds and took his title.

It should have been the end, but three years later, when he was 40, Fitzsimmons had another terrific scrap with Jeffries, losing in eight rounds this time. By 1903, when he was 41, the light heavyweight division had been introduced and Ruby Robert won and held this for two more years. His last recorded fight was in 1914 when he was 52 years old. He was the most remarkable fighter of his time, perhaps of all time.

BOMBARDIER BILLY WELLS
(1889 — 1967)

The true story of the way Bombardier Billy Wells came into professional boxing would, if written as fiction, totally destroy the credibility of its author. At the age of nineteen, fresh off a boat from India where he had won an army championship - "Bombardier" was no flashy nickname invented by a publicist, it was his rank, equivalent to Corporal - he walked into an office just off the Strand in London. It was the business premises of a great sporting journal, *Boxing*, forerunner of today's *Boxing News*, and here it was suggested that he might like a private trial against, of all people, the reigning British Heavyweight Champion, Gunner Moir. Wells, 6 feet 3 inches and weighing 13½ stone, happily accepted.

For a full two rounds he did well, bouncing around up on his toes, shooting what was to remain throughout his career as his best punch - an impeccable left jab. It bounced off the stockier, slower but more muscular and menacing champion fifty or so times in those six minutes but, ominously, only increased a mounting irritation in the target. Wells simply was not in any sort of physical condition after a long and rough sea passage in a packed troopship. In the third round a left hook to the body bent him over, brought his chin in range and a right cross knocked him spark out. When he came round he said, "I can see now that professional boxing is very different from army boxing." But, quite rightly, it did not deter him.

He quickly built up a string of victories, mainly with that left hand. It was always much more than a speculative prod. It was a hurtful, accurate punch, thrown arrow straight with lightning speed, and it was the reason Wells was never once outpointed in a career that lasted almost sixteen years and numbered almost 60 fights.

Wells was the first genuine public idol - wide-shouldered, deep-chested, narrow-waisted, marvellously handsome. He was a sculptor's dream, the best-built British Heavyweight Champion before Joe Bugner, and he was totally unmarked when he retired. He held the British heavyweight title for just over nine years, from 1911 to 1919 – a record until Henry Cooper broke it in the 1970s – and actually defended it successfully even more often than Henry, thirteen times. That should have earned him four Lonsdale belts and set a prouder record than even Cooper's three.

In those days, however, Lonsdale belts were awarded only for contests in the snobbish, dinner-jacketed, members only, "no cheering during the rounds" National Sporting Club. Other venues paid more, but if a fighter wanted glory he had to take less money at the NSC. That is why Wells won only one of the much prized paunch adornments. Bombardier Billy's popularity demanded bigger audiences and that appeal remained defiantly undiminished when he lost one of those early fights to the same Gunner Moir, by then an ex-champion, in circumstances similar to their first unofficial behind-closed-doors private fight. Wells, stronger and fitter by then, hit Moir so hard and so often in the first couple of rounds he punched himself out. He simply had not built up sufficient stamina and when Moir went to work on the body Billy collapsed and was counted out. It was the first worrying indication of a weakness that was to haunt him horribly – but not yet. When he stepped up his training he went

Some idea of Bombardier Billy's size, style and unmarked good looks are there in a training picture at the end of his career.

twenty rounds to beat a seasoned pro, Porky Flynn, and was ready at the age of 21 for the great Iron Hague, winner in one round over Billy's so far solitary conqueror, Gunner Moir. Hague, at the time, was a very hot favourite.

Wells was outstanding that night at the NSC, outsmarting and outpunching Hague, and seemingly answering one query by surviving solid head punches to knock his man out in the sixth round. Reviews in *Boxing* could only be called ecstatic and that from a journal that was proud of its reputation as the sport's bible. The same editor who once doubted whether Wells would ever be strong enough to be a champion now hoped that he could develop into "one of the very best men the world had ever seen". He wrote quite seriously about the Bombardier's chances against the legendary World Heavyweight Champion: "Johnson boxes on retreat and tries to coax his opponents to come after him. Wells is long enough in the arm to reach him . . . Given the necessary strength and stamina and a little more experience of possible dangers Wells should stand a good chance."

Doubts – and reality – started to creep back in the following year when Bombardier Billy Wells had three fights in America. He outboxed and knocked out Tom Kennedy, reputed at the time to be an independently wealthy millionaire, which hints at a slightly eccentric playboy opponent. He punched so hard against another, Al Palzer, that a 16-stone giant of a man was lifted off his feet – but still got up to stop Wells with body punches. A better known fighter, Gunboat Smith, stopped him in two rounds.

But if that was a bad year, 1913 was to become a disaster – and if that seems an overstatement one report about Georges Carpentier's fourth-round knock-out of Wells at Ghent was described by a sportswriter of the time as being adequate French revenge for the defeat, almost a hundred years earlier, of Napoleon by Wellington. On reflection, maybe it was. Carpentier was only nineteen, with the looks and the physique of a schoolboy even though he had been boxing professionally at fourteen. Wells towered over him, half a head taller, 19 lbs heavier, built like a Greek god. It seemed almost unfair when, in the first round, he rammed home that left and cracked across a right to put the Frenchman down. Wells could, in fact, claim that he knocked out Carpentier, because it was a disgracefully slow count, estimated by independent stop watches at almost twelve seconds, though Carpentier listened to it on one knee from five and got up at nine. He was down again in the second round, but, so the story goes, had carried the fight to Wells throughout the third, digging so effectively to the body that he told his corner at the start of the fourth, "Now I shall knock him out." Another

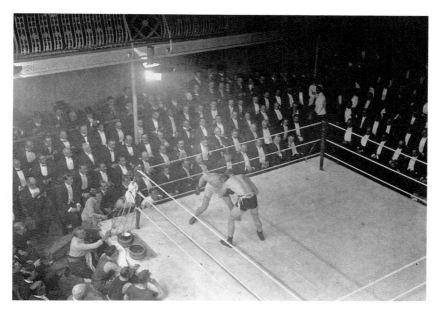

*Georges Carpentier is just about to swing a devastating blow to the
Bombardier's body at the NSC.*

flurry of hooks to the ribs did just that.

Wells did regain some credibility by knocking out his old adversary,
Gunner Moir, three months later and people were beginning to believe
the story that he had been ill before the fight against Carpentier. It was
preferable in those nationalistic days to accepting that the pride of
England had been deservedly conquered by an undersized effete
Frenchman. The return fight at the National Sporting Club in December
had the whole country's honour at stake. There were attempts to
unsettle Carpentier before it started. A policeman appeared in his
dressing room to warn that manslaughter charges could result.
Carpentier did not understand and an interpreter told him the officer
had come to wish him luck. Wells kept him waiting five minutes in the
ring and then tried to protest about the bandages on his hand. Exactly
seventy three seconds later Carpentier had him writhing on the floor
from a right to the head and a left to the body – punches few even saw.
The referee actually had to issue an official indignant statement that
blows had definitely been struck. The crowd yelled "fake" and
"coward".

It is a sad fact that a decent, sporting man who went on to perform for
more than five years as British Champion never lived down the events of
that nightmare.

BRUCE WOODCOCK
(1 9 2 1 —   )

Bruce Woodcock had everything required to become that comparative rarity, a genuine 24-carat world-class heavyweight – except the right advice. That is the inescapable conclusion of an examination of the record and performances of a fighter who in his day attracted the excited attention of soccer-sized crowds and yet finished up as "the man who could not quite". There are those who argue still that, properly handled and promoted, he could have become the greatest heavyweight prospect this country has produced. And no one should doubt that the grooming of young heavyweights is desperately important. Henry Cooper and Joe Bugner were not the only ones who were steered gingerly clear of too dangerous opposition in their formative years. It happened to world champions like Rocky Marciano and Floyd Patterson among others.

Bruce Woodcock, at eighteen in 1939, was Amateur Light Heavyweight Champion, a stylist in an attractive orthodox fashion. As a young professional during World War II he put on muscle working as a fitter in the railway yards of his native Doncaster and gained steady experience while the more significant fighting was going on all round the globe. By the time peace returned to Europe he had built a string of victories against reasonable opponents and at the age of 24, 6 feet tall and weighing 14 stone, was just the size and shape of hero the fans of Britain, starved of much big-time boxing, were hungry to acclaim. Almost 40,000 people packed into White Hart Lane, Tottenham, to see his challenge for the British and Empire Heavyweight titles in July 1945.

The titles had been won a year earlier by 32-year-old Jack London, who, though paunchy and balding, had been too ponderously invulnerable for a more than three stone lighter Freddie Mills. London found Woodcock a very different proposition, however – when he was able to find him. Lumbering and outclassed, he spent most of the first five rounds being peppered with left jabs and then, in the sixth, Woodcock's always punishing right cross found a gap and it was all over.

The following year, completely overestimating Woodcock's still-raw talent, his manager Tom Hurst took him to New York. Against all advice, Hurst accepted a fight for him with a rough, tough up-and-coming ambitious young heavyweight, Tami Mauriello. When Woodcock outboxed him Tami tried another way, a savage head-butt, and the half-blinded badly cut young hopeful was knocked out. An indication of how highly Mauriello was rated was that his own next fight was for the World Heavyweight title against the great Joe Louis, who stopped him inside a round.

It was further proof of how short-sighted promoters could be that only seventeen days later Bruce Woodcock was pitted against his main rival as a serious attraction – the reigning Light Heavyweight Champion, Freddie Mills, who himself had only the previous month been knocked out in a savage world title fight by Gus Lesnevich. Woodcock, however, won handsomely over ten rounds. He always did have the measure of the game and, Freddie's face-first style suited Bruce perfectly.

On the Continent in the immediate post-war years, talent was even more thinly spread than in Britain. The European Heavyweight title, held in 1939 by the great German boxer, Max Schmeling, had been abandoned by him after injuries he suffered in Crete as a paratrooper in the Wehrmacht. A Swede and a Belgian briefly disputed it, but it was vacant again when it was decided that a Frenchman, Albert Renet, had the credentials to fight Woodcock for it. They were wrong. Once Woodcock recovered from the surprise of discovering Renet was a southpaw he knocked him out with that potent right cross in six.

But once again he was disastrously overmatched in 1947 against Joe Baksi, a giant American, whom all the world's top contenders for Joe Louis's title were carefully avoiding. The first punch of the fight broke Woodcock's jaw, starting investigations into a ridiculous story that the huge and amiable Baksi had, outside the ring, reinforced his fist with a metal object covered in leather to match his gloves. Woodcock fought on for another seven rounds before he was stopped, though he remembered nothing after that first shattering punch.

The promoters found him an easier American to fight in 1948 – in fact, disgracefully easy. An ex-convict, Lee Oma should have been locked up again for the way he rolled over and played dead in the fourth round, with the crowd shouting to the rhythm of Big Ben's chimes, "Lay down, lay down, lay down, lay down". In the same year another American, Lee Savold, turned out to be too dirty a fighter and was disqualified for a low punch.

Two years later when they met again in 1950, an open-air promotion at The White City, the British Boxing Board of Control actually went

Lesnevich was rated a master boxer, but Woodcock was convincingly ahead on points before stopping him in eight rounds.

along with manager Jack Solomons in declaring the fight to be for the world title vacated by the immortal Joe Louis. Woodcock had been out of action for almost a full year after flattening Freddie Mills in fourteen rounds in June 1949. Savold had not fought anyone since December 1948. But once again the American proved himself too rough and tough for Woodcock, who had never been quite the same since the Baksi fight. This time he was cut and stopped in four rounds. The British Board did, in fact, vainly try to pretend recognition of the 34-year-old Savold, but that hollow mockery was quietly abandoned when Louis, during an attempted comeback at the age of 37, cut Savold to pieces in June 1951, six months before he too was forced into permanent retirement by a certain Rocky Marciano.

Retirement was all that was left for Woodcock after he dropped his British and Empire titles to a stiff, awkward Guardsman, Jack Gardner, who once would never have lived with him, but at least it was a healthy retirement to a pub in his beloved Yorkshire and a less punishing game to conquer – golf.

Bruce Woodcock just missed with this left, but he always landed often enough to be too good for the smaller and lighter Freddie Mills.

DON COCKELL
(1928 — 83)

When fight fans remember Don Cockell, the conversations invariably concentrate on the brutal beating he took in the Kezar Stadium, San Francisco, from World Heavyweight Champion Rocky Marciano, the man who thought the rule book was for cissies. If some of the criminal acts committed against the brave Englishman that night had taken place in the street Rocky would have been arrested. Yet there is an even more cruel injustice to Cockell in the blow dealt to him by a fate that robbed him of what those who know feel was his true destiny. He should have had a place in history as one of the great light heavyweights of all time, very probably a world champion in the division where he truly belonged.

He won the British title, vacated by Freddie Mills, at the age of 22 when, after a grim pursuit of Mark Hart, he finally caught up with his man and put him down four times before stopping him in the fourteenth round. He added the European title a year later, battering a Frenchman, Albert Yvel, in seven rounds. He was heading for the top, a man with all the traditional strength of his first trade as a blacksmith and blessed with natural talent, a solid left jab and a repertoire that, although unspectacular, had every punch in the book. Suddenly and inexplicably, however, something went wrong with his metabolism. Everything he ate or drank turned to fat on a 5 feet 10 inch frame. Trying to boil that weight off by starving and sweating was no way to defend his crown against the great Randolph Turpin. It is a minor miracle he survived as long as he did – into the eleventh round of a one-sided affair and knocked down three times before the referee rescued him in June 1952.

Cockell went into hospital for tests that resulted in specialists telling him that he would have to settle for carrying the burden of excess weight for the rest of his life. At the age of 24 he seemed finished as a fighter. But Cockell remembered how he and a stable-mate, Jack Gardner, used to spar regularly when Gardner, several inches taller and more than 2 stone heavier, was British Heavyweight Champion. "I remembered how easily

Cockell moves inside a Williams left jab to launch one of the left hooks to the body that won the British Heavyweight title.

I handled him and how regularly I outpointed him even if it was only in the gymnasium," said Cockell. "And I reckoned I still had a future as a heavyweight."

Few others did, although the division was woefully short of talent at the time. Johnny Williams, a superb boxer with a classic style, was Champion and the only other semi-serious contender at the time was the ageing Tommy Farr, forced by financial circumstances into a comeback when he was close to 40. Tommy by then was fighting mainly from memory – though, of course, he still remembered more than most had ever learned.

The British Boxing Board refused to recognise Cockell v. Farr as a final eliminator, saying they would reserve judgement until afterwards. In the event Cockell so dominated the once-great Welshman that the referee stopped the fight after seven totally one-sided rounds. Cockell received a nod of grudging approval from the Board that he bitterly resented – and two months later he stepped in as a distinct second favourite against the Champion. The crowd even laughed when his weight was announced – 14 stone 9 lbs and too much of it fat. From the start he went after Williams, thumping in tremendous left hooks to the body and advancing non-stop, wading through the famous Williams jabs so relentlessly that by the end of the fight both his eyes had been cut and closed. Cockell had to be led back to the dressing room, but the Lonsdale belt was around his waist and an astonishing heavyweight career was off the ground, into orbit.

He travelled to America to outbox Harry "Kid" Matthews, high in the rankings as a contender. He travelled to South Africa to win on points against the home-based Johnny Arthur in Johannesburg, where local boys never lost unless they were licked out of sight. Most significantly he also outpointed Roland La Starza, another rated American and a superb boxer with his own special claim to fame. He had gone the distance once with Rocky Marciano and had lasted eleven rounds in a return match with the title at stake.

Cockell had arrived as a genuine contender with a belief in his ability to do well against Marciano even after going to the cinema to watch a film of Rocky slaughtering Ezzard Charles. He said, "They ought to give that one an X certificate to stop youngsters getting bad boxing habits. He butted Charles, hit him after the bell and the last punch that put him

Cockells and hidden muscles. Don returns to his hotel after a training run before the Marciano fight. With him is his wife, Irene.

Cockell, weakened by taking off weight is in early trouble against Turpin as he loses his British Light Heavyweight title.

down landed smack on the back of his neck. But I still say that the man who does beat Rocky will have the same style as me. You've got to jab him hard and often. Give him a moment's rest and he is after you again."

Later, just before he set off for the Marciano fight he revealed another part of his game plan. "If he butts me I'll nut him back. If he hits me low, I'll hit him lower. If he lands after the bell, I'll do the same." Cockell tried to keep his word. He did particularly well with his stinging left jab in the first couple of rounds, but then, as the *New York World Telegram* reported, "Marciano violated practically every rule in the book. He hit after the bell, used his elbows and head in close quarters, several times punched below the belt and once hit Cockell when he was down." The referee finally stopped the fight at the end of the ninth round. What happened to the rest of the game? Why didn't Cockell be equally as dirty? He said simply, "To Marciano it came naturally. To me it didn't. I had to think about doing it and by then the chance had gone."

Something else had gone too – because like so many others Cockell was never quite the same fighter again. He retired the following year, 1956, after being stopped by a crude big-punching Tongan, Kitione Lave, a man his class entitled him to spank.

HENRY COOPER
(1934 —)

There are youngsters around today who are in danger of growing up believing that Henry Cooper threw only one great left hook in his life - the punch that dropped, hurt and almost knocked out Cassius Clay, before he became Muhammad Ali, at Wembley in May 1963. There are others who could be guilty of believing that Henry's most important fight against a British opponent was his last, when, at the age of 37, in March 1971, he had his titles taken from him by 21-year-old Joe Bugner, or - if you feel, as Henry does - by referee Harry Gibbs. He has always believed he won the fight clearly and feels a totally uncharacteristic bitter resentment about the result.

There are, in fact, many myths about Henry's career, including the one that the main reason he lost fights was because the flesh around his eyes split open too easily. He was cut often, but only four of his 55 fights were stopped for that reason and two of those were against Ali. It is just one of the very many tributes to his total professionalism that he learned to live with the blood that flowed in many of his fights. For most of them he allowed one of the men in his corner, trainer Danny Holland, to repair the damage, forgot about it and got on with the job. In truth it was probably his perfect dedication and determination, allied of course to a considerable talent, that makes him a strong contender for this century's outstanding British Heavyweight Champion.

Cooper won the title in January 1959 and held it until the Bugner fight -apart from a brief spell in those twelve years when, angered by a Board of Control decision to withhold world title recognition from a proposed fight against Jimmy Ellis for a WBA crown, he relinquished it to register his disgust.

In between he defended the title often enough to win three Lonsdale belts, a unique achievement. During his reign he saw off two generations of talent. First there was Joe Erskine, Brian London and Dick Richardson - with cagey, clever Erskine the only one who bothered him for a spell, until Henry stopped him three times in a row. Then there were the younger men coming up: Johnny Prescott, Jack Bodell and Billy Walker. He disposed of all three without too much bother, even though the years were catching up on him.

Henry will always give a large slice of the credit for that to his famous manager, wise and wily Jim Wicks, a man worth a book on his own and certainly meriting a chapter in Henry's life story. They called Jim "The Bishop" and no one ever knew why, though there was a theory that in one argument over money Harry Levene was thought to have shouted at him, "Go unfrock yourself". The basis of this relationship with Henry and twin brother George, who also fought professionally as Jim Cooper, was trust. Henry first met "Mr Wicks", as he was to call him respectfully for years, when he won the ABA Light Heavyweight title. He might have turned pro then, but his future manager advised him to wait until after National Service although he risked losing Henry to less scrupulous representatives, of whom boxing has never been short. Jim's reasoning was that, as a professional, Henry would not be eligible to box for the Army. As it happened Henry did very little soldiering during his two years. He was quickly snapped up by the Ordnance Corps, famous for its boxing team, and found that the RSM was a man he had once knocked out.

There were other, less obvious, advantages in having Jim Wicks in charge of his young career. A manager who pays a prospect is inclined to look for a quick return on his money. The only question he is likely to ask is how much his share of the purse will be. It was Wicks's policy to leave his 25 per cent unclaimed until the prize-money topped £100 and he would not allow Henry to fight anyone who was unsuitable as an opponent. The first contract between them was for three years and it was never officially renewed. Mutual trust, respect and affection kept them as a team throughout Henry's career – yet ironically the time the contract was due for re-signing coincided with the worst spell in Cooper's career. He was stopped on cuts by the journeyman Peter Bates, knocked out by Joe Bygraves for the Empire title, by Ingemar Johanneson for the European crown and outpointed by Joe Erskine in a British title fight. It was the faith of Jim Wicks that persuaded him to carry on, especially when the promoters were not queuing up for his talents. He had to have three fights in Germany for a comeback, but proved he was all the way back by beating Dick Richardson with a clean one-punch KO, and outpointing a highly rated American, Zora Folley. By this stage Henry had learned, among other things, what was his ideal fighting weight. There are those who imagine that a heavyweight is OK if, at the weigh-in, he is alive and sober, but the matter of weight can be crucial. Henry found that his best weight was just over 13½ stone and for most of his career set out to achieve that with dedicated training methods.

Cooper, cut as usual, outpointed the top contender, Zora Folley of America. He just missed with this right swing.

Outside the ring he has always had a justified reputation as a genuinely nice man, cheerful, honest, good tempered, witty and warm. Inside it he could be mean, including with sparring partners who were well paid and made to earn their money. The left hook was already becoming famous even before he put Clay down with it in that dramatic fourth round – which must be seen in perspective.

Clay was still a comparative novice of 21 at the time, seemingly intent on clowning until the fifth round arrived. It was the one in which he had "predicted" he would win. It almost never arrived for him at all. Henry had Clay down and stunned when the bell went at the end of the fourth – another half minute was as much as he probably needed to finish the job. But another minute and a half elapsed, with a replacement glove being sought for the one Clay had split, giving the flashy youngster precious extra rest. He then cut and slashed Cooper so badly that the fight had to be stopped.

Henry's greatest moment. He has just left-hooked Cassius Clay to the canvas and those eyes tell their significant story.

Henry looks as fed up as he felt when the 21-year-old Joe Bugner is named as the points winner and new champion.

Henry was entering the veteran stage by then, but on into his thirties he was still capable of letting that famous left hook explode on opposing chins. He could not, however, land it on a vastly improved Muhammad Ali, who again cut him savagely when the world title was at stake in May 1966. And now boxing was taking more out of him. Not the fights themselves, it must be emphasised, but the punishing routines he knew he had to endure to be in top shape for those fights.

That was why he had made up his mind to retire even before he stepped in against Bugner. Maybe it made it all the harder for him to take – yet strangely it increased his public popularity enormously. He has been able to command large fees since for advertising, public appearances and after dinner speaking. He has been shrewdly advised on investments, yet he will always appear for nothing for charity or to do a favour for a friend. Henry will always be a man who needs no crown to be a king among his countrymen.

*There could be no arguments when referee Tommy Little decided that
Cooper was too badly cut to be allowed to continue against Clay.*

JOE BUGNER
(1 9 5 0 —   )

Joe Bugner was the best equipped English heavyweight of all time. He was also, despite his detractors, one of the most accomplished heavyweight champions in the history of the British Isles – at his best. He had just about everything: the physique, the jab, the defence, the strength, the willingness to work hard, even occasionally the punch. The only thing he ever lacked, apart from in occasional flashes, was the love of the sport itself that produces chilling ferocity.

Incidentally, anyone who wants to argue that Bugner should not be described as English because he was born in Hungary should remember that England would have been glad, grateful and proud to claim him for her own if he had won the world title for which he challenged. Now an Australian citizen, he no longer pretends any great love for the country that he once called home but then perhaps he is entitled to feel that he was given no convincing reason to do so. He never completely captured British hearts and imaginations even very early in his career when as a teenager he took over Billy Walker's "Golden Boy" title – without having to fight for it. Right from his early days he had critics and fans divided into different camps. There were many who saw him as an ambling, amiable robot, jerked around on a very short leash by a manager, Andy Smith, who let him off occasionally to box strictly to orders against carefully chosen opponents who would not do much damage. There were the enthusiasts, so desperate for someone to fulfil their own dreams of heavyweight glory that they invested him with too much hope, too much ambition –and turned even more viciously against him in the end.

There was also a slight majority of those who saw him as a genuinely exciting prospect. For a long time they were prepared to recognise that because he had hardly had an amateur career, did not lace on gloves until he was seventeen, was knocked out in his first paid fight and, despite his huge size was immature and inarticulate, it did need time. The ingredients of ability and dedication have to be cooked at the right temperature. But even his most fervent supporters began to feel after twenty fights that the careful choice of opponents was becoming irksome. Even though he needed the armour of experience before being taken out of cotton wool, some of the human obstacles put in front of him performed more like stepping stones. They belonged not so much in boxing's "Who's Who" as "Who's That?".

But gradually, around his twentieth year, the sights were set higher. Men such as Brian London, Johnny Prescott, Eduardo Corletti and Chuck Wepner were beaten, and a few days after his 21st birthday Joe was pronounced ready for the big one - for the British, Commonwealth and European heavyweight crowns held by the legendary, much loved Henry Cooper. Joe's upset victory did him no favour after a fight that still creates controversy. He boxed intelligently, but even though some had forecast Joe's success it was generally still felt that Henry had done just enough. Harry Gibbs did not, however, and his verdict was the one that mattered. The biggest irony is that Gibbs was recognised then, and

The worst night – and worst fight – of Joe Bugner's career, when Jack Bodell dethroned him.

*Joe Bugner managed to look and sound menacing before his last fight.
Bruno, as usual, looked impassive.*

rightly still is, as one of the greatest, strictest, most completely unbiased referees in history. Some people never forgave Joe Bugner.

He almost threw it all away with the only thoroughly shoddy and substandard performance of his whole career when he blew those titles six months later to Jack Bodell, a man not remotely in his class, a southpaw he had flattened as a sparring partner. Yet a year later there were real signs of a sleeping giant at last coming to life. He regained and twice defended the European title and beat a couple of useful Americans, including a former WBA World Heavyweight Champion, Jimmy Ellis. Within another six months he became the only Englishman and one of the few of any nationality to go the full twelve rounds with Muhammad Ali, who was at the time waiting to regain the World Heavyweight title. Survival was creditable for Joe, still only 22, particularly as he had been cut over the left eye in the first round for the first time in his life – but it had to be conceded that he wanted to win only credit, not an earth-shattering result.

Yet six months later when he took on another truly great ex-world champ, the awesome Joe Frazier, a man who pounded on opponents with a drum-beat rhythm that came from a genuine fighting heart, Bugner gave the performance of his life. Knocked down and badly hurt in

Bugner looked a genuine world title contender when he went close to an
upset victory over the great "Smokin'" Joe Frazier.

the tenth round by that famous left hook, he fought back so ferociously that had it been a fifteen-round fight instead of twelve he might easily have won. Frazier was half-blinded by a bruised and closed left eye at the end and the fight might even have been stopped.

Bugner continued his winning ways until at the age of 25, at the peak of his physical power and with nearly sixty professional fights to give him that armour of experience, he promised he felt capable of taking the world title from champion again Muhammad Ali in Kuala Lumpur in 1975. He broke that promise. Survival became once again the name of the game and from that Malayan ringside spectators could confirm that a typographical error in the Press Association report got it exactly right. It started, "Joe Bugner lost a fifteen round flight against Muhammad Ali . . .".

Disillusioned, Joe quit the game temporarily the following year. You could say he retired hurt. He did come back to prove a point and demolish Richard Dunn in a single savage round the following autumn and there have been comebacks of varying success subsequently, including an Indian Summer in Australia against some useful Americans such as James Tillis, Greg Page and David Bey. But Joe was getting older and slower, even if he at least and at last learned how to talk a good fight. It all ended almost abjectly in a comprehensive defeat by Frank Bruno in 1987. But there are those with valid reasons for claiming that for a Bugner at his best that result might have been different.

It is all over. Joe Bugner retired after his fight against Bruno, but did so virtually unmarked.

*Cut for the first time in his career, against Ali, in Las Vegas, Bugner still
lasted the full twelve rounds.*

FRANK BRUNO
(1 9 6 1 —   )

Frank Bruno's fans claim that his monstrous physique, his jolting jab and murderous finishing punch make him the greatest English heavyweight of all time. That futile argument will have to remain to be discussed elsewhere - getting hotter by the minute, with the fans of Cooper, Bugner, and other great fighters joining in. No man can achieve more than to become the very best of his own time and Bruno certainly climbed that peak.

His manager Terry Lawless has always seen him on top of another more important mountain. The man to whom Bruno was introduced as a shy 21 year old in 1983 was precisely what Lawless always hoped Frank would eventually become, a man who was a rich, respected, cultured, dignified ex-World Heavyweight Champion who was also incidentally black - Floyd Patterson. Bruno had already earned some of those attributes though he was born with only one - the colour of his skin. He was always big as a boy and might even have become bad until, at twelve, the youngest of six children, he was sent away to what was diplomatically called a "special school". Natural aggression, which is now barely credible to anyone who meets the warm and gentle person outside the ring, was channelled so successfully into boxing that by the age of eighteen he was ABA Heavyweight Champion. He had to endure a series of eye operations before he was ready to turn professional in 1982 at the age of 21 - which reinforced all Lawless's natural determination to protect magnificent raw material. He said at the time: "Frank Bruno hasn't had more than forty rounds of boxing in his life. If he gets pushed too soon it could be disastrous."

Frank's first fourteen fights in thirteen months lasted an average of a few seconds over two rounds. Just the sight of Bruno's huge frame coming out of an opposite corner was enough to half-paralyse some of the opposition and, although the fans loved it, they also, perversely, wanted to see him taken longer distances by harder men who might hurt him. Their attitude ignored significant factors. One was that all the

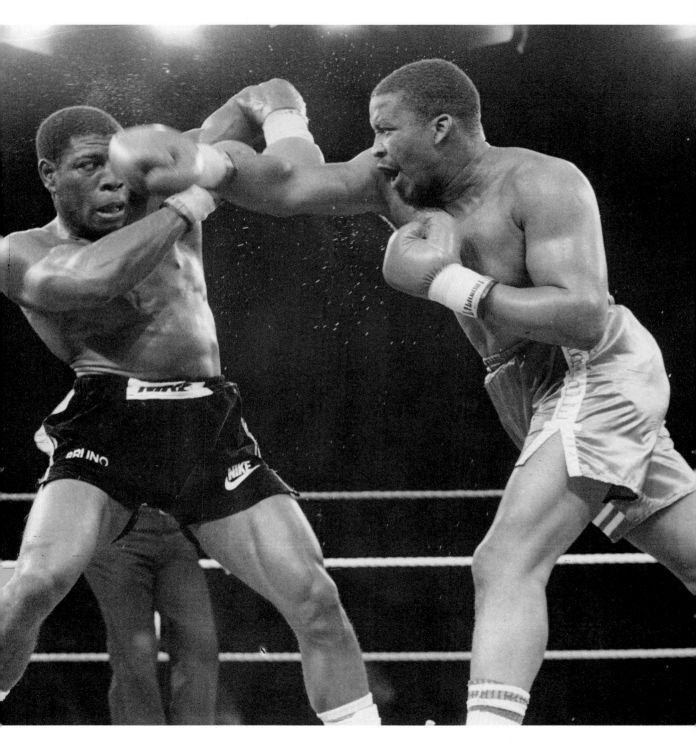

Against Tim Witherspoon, Bruno had the height, the physique and the punch, but it was the American champion who had the durability.

modern great heavyweights from Joe Louis onwards, Marciano and Muhammad Ali included, were brought on as carefully and slowly. In even earlier times men fought for years to gain the experience necessary to achieve championship class. Another danger was that had Bruno knocked over a big name too early in his career, he would have been boosted immediately into a higher class long before he was ready. That was, perhaps, why an ideal teaching opponent, Joe Bugner, who was making one of his many comebacks around that time, was always ignored – until much later. Scott Ledoux, whom Bruno beat in his fifteenth fight, did represent a step up in class because this American had at one time been a top contender. Ledoux had fought five World Championship claimants – George Foreman, Larry Holmes, Mike Weaver, Ken Norton and Leon Spinks – and had drawn with the last two. But by then Ledoux was 34, rich and contented. He was knocked down by a left hook in the first round, cut in the second, battered and stopped in the third.

It was mainly for learning experience in the tougher atmosphere of American gyms that Bruno crossed the Atlantic for a spell in 1983 but it helped with the costs when he ended the trip with a fight in Chicago against Mike Jameson, a Californian with neither the credentials nor even the ambition to test him – but it was still significant because it was after this one that there was a shift in the Lawless–Bruno relationship. Bruno ended the fight in the second round that July day with two totally efficient punches, a left hook that cut Jameson's brow to the bone, dropping him on to a right uppercut that made counting over his body a formality. Said Lawless: "Frank has now matured enough to have a say in all the decisions. From now on it is a partnership. That finish showed me that all the lessons he has been learning in seventy rounds against top men have clicked into place. He is ready for top class opposition."

Another very wise man, Angelo Dundee, had more cautious counsel. He advised Lawless: "Don't let anyone hustle or rush you. You are doing everything right with Bruno. He is shaping well, but he ain't there yet. He still has a tendency to walk forward, when he should be gliding in and out." It brought back something Floyd Patterson had said after meeting Bruno, taking a liking to him – and watching him fight. "The kid can go all the way. The left jab is beautiful, but he still has a lot to learn. For instance, if he is going to be World Champion, he is going to be hurt at some stage. He has to know how to get up, pretend he isn't hurt, kid an opponent."

That is a stratagem Bruno was dangerously slow to learn and it brought him close to disaster in a fight at the Albert Hall in October 1983. In the first round a looping right from a massive heavy puncher, Jumbo Cummings, whirled in like a grenade and smashed against the

Bruno was battered down in a corner in the eleventh round against Witherspoon and the referee moves in to stop it.

side of Bruno's head. He was out on his feet, stiff as a board, so much a target that another punch might have wrecked him, when the bell saved him. Lawless half-dragged, half-carried him to the corner and the second round became a struggle for survival.

Bruno's critics somehow do not remember quite as clearly that, with his head clear, he punched Cummings to a standstill by the seventh round and with that win achieved his first world ranking – at number ten in the World Boxing Association list. He seemed all set to progress steadily up those ratings until the fight against another would-be contender, James "Bonecrusher" Smith, at Wembley in May 1984. The American was just as big and an inch taller at 6 feet 4 inches. Bruno mastered him so competently for most of the ten rounds that he needed only to keep his hands up and box. But, as he said, he "wanted to tear his head off", went in aggressively and walked into a left hook to the temple. If he had gone down, taken a count, given himself time to think, he could still have won. Instead he sagged into the ropes, his hands down, his head exposed for the dozen punches that Smith, with adrenalin pumping, smashed at him. This time when Bruno went down he could not beat the count. It looked as though the idol had a chin of clay, but his first words in an interview afterwards were a meaningful, "I'll be back". He was still only 22 and a bigger cloud on his immediate horizon was Terry Lawless's very real threat to retire in disappointment. The manager said, "Maybe I don't take those punches in the head, but they do hit me in the heart." It was Bruno who persuaded Lawless that the partnership still had places to go and the rehabilitation process did not, in fact, take too long.

After four build-up victories to restore the faith in British fans, who traditionally yearn for heavyweight heroes, the master-stroke was the fight that made Bruno European Heavyweight Champion, a four-round demolition job on a giant Swede, Anders Eklund, in October 1985. It was a title Lawless had earlier firmly shunned – for the same reason that he never pointed Bruno at the British Championship Frank could undoubtedly have dominated. Lawless reasons, "It takes too much control out of the hands of the manager, into the committee rooms. They can tell a champion who and when he has to fight when it is the world title that Frank Bruno was always aimed at."

Still, the European crown helped to re-establish Frank in the rankings. So did a sensational one-round knock-out victory over the former WBA World Champion Gerry Coetzee. The South African had been a very considerable fighter, but Bruno was back to his most menacing for that Wembley one-punch win in March 1986.

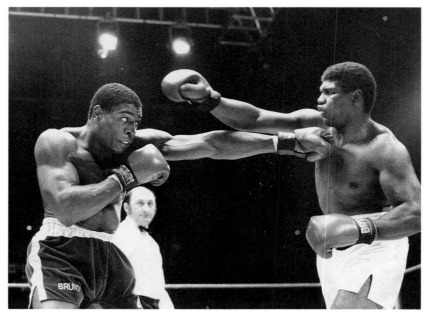

Bruno battled his way into the ratings by outboxing and stopping the flashy James "Quick" Tillis.

In his early days they fed Bruno a few victims and this one, Jeff Jordan of the USA, was stopped in three rounds.

Bruno made a memorable first attempt on Tim Witherspoon's WBA World title in the open air at Wembley in July 1986 and was in front by the seventh round, moving towards the second half of the fight. But the giant American, impregnable even to some solid shots, steamed on relentlessly, increasing his own pressure. In the eleventh a long right smashed Bruno to the ropes and, yet again, inexperience, when hurt, proved catastrophic. Witherspoon flailed away at him powerfully and mercilessly and the towel came fluttering in as the referee stopped it.

There are those who have reservations about Bruno's promotion to the rating of number one challenger by both WBC and WBA, which earned him the automatic right to be next in line to meet the man who unified the world heavyweight situation as undisputed Champion, Mike Tyson. But Tyson eliminated virtually every other contender and Bruno kept himself impressively fit and ready through the frustrations of many postponements. He also avoided any further defeats after the Witherspoon fight – though that did not overtax his resources. He had four wins all inside the distance – over James "Quick" Tillis, the disgracefully over-matched Chuck Gardner, a hopelessly outclassed Reggie Cross and then, in October 1987, what was left of an ageing Joe Bugner.

It is more important that when the chance finally arrives again Frank Bruno promises, "I will be ready".

LEN HARVEY

(1 9 0 7 — 7 6)

One small but very telling fact says a great deal about Len Harvey, a man whose career spanned not only 22 years but every weight division from flyweight to heavyweight, even though he was never more than a light heavyweight. It is that during the literally thousands of rounds he sparred he never wore a headguard. He also, in hundreds of fights, more than three hundred, never wore what all boxers today consider an absolute essential, a gum-shield. Harvey felt that he was a sufficient master of the defensive skills of boxing to need neither. And the statistics alone provide incontrovertible evidence of how right he was. When he was knocked out in his 35th year by the immensely strong 22-year-old Freddie Mills to lose his British and Empire cruiserweight titles in 1942 it was only the second time in all those years, all those fights, that he lost inside the distance. The other time was when Jack Petersen temporarily blinded him in regaining the British heavyweight title in 1934.

There will never be another quite like Len Harvey. That is not merely an appreciation of his talent but a statement of fact because, for a start, he was a professional fighter before his thirteenth birthday, while he was still at school. He was paid five shillings – 25p, an amount that would be scorned as pocket money by that age-group nowadays – and would hand over his wages to his mother in those far-off hard-up days. It would not, could not, be permitted nowadays.

He had his first eight-round fight at the age of fourteen and by the time he was sixteen was good enough to try his hand in London, fighting regularly over fifteen two-minute rounds, once over twenty rounds. Most of those fights went the distance against older and vastly more experienced men, with young Len becoming an increasingly popular favourite with fans who liked his upstanding style. Years later, one of those experienced older men, Ernie Jarvis, who was good enough to fight for the world flyweight title, confirmed that he was very much more than a left jabber with a good defence. Ernie, who became boxing writer for *The People*, told the story of how on the way to a fifteen-rounds points

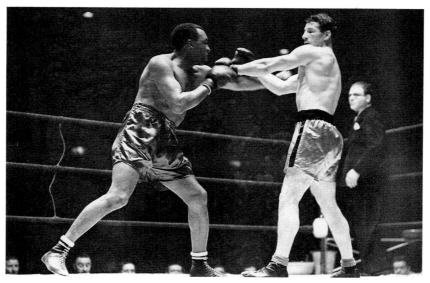

*Larry Gains, the black Canadian, was big, strong, brave and experienced,
but still could not get through the Harvey defence.*

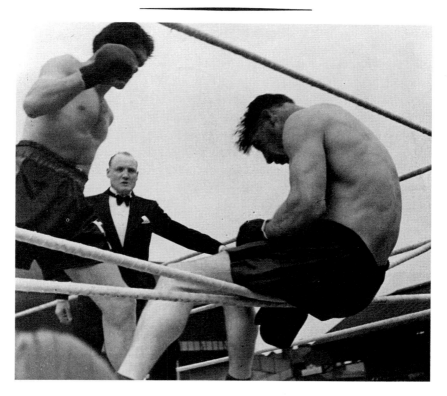

*Harvey is on his way out of the ring and out of boxing as the youth, strength
and fitness of Mills prove too much.*

One of his finest hours, Len ties up World Champion John Henry Lewis but could not take his title.

defeat at The Ring, Blackfriars, Harvey, then sixteen, knocked him down by a left hook. To the end of his life Jarvis maintained it was the hardest punch he ever took in a long career.

By the time Harvey was eighteen, he had grown into a full welterweight, regularly topping the bill, fighting once, twice, sometimes three times in a month – again unheard of nowadays. But there were still those who felt it was premature when, at eighteen, he fought the clever and tricky Harry Mason over twenty rounds at The Albert Hall for the British welterweight title. Harvey's own attitude was typical – "You get nowhere and learn nothing from fighting mugs" –and his reaction to his first appearance at an intimidating venue was coolly similar. He was at home in a boxing ring anywhere, against anyone. Mason was 23, winner of most of 84 fights, including six for the title, and was a top-class performer in his own right.

Harvey knocked him down twice, in the first and eighteenth rounds of a fascinating fight, packed with dramatic shifts in fortune and many thought he was unlucky to get only a draw. Harvey did not complain – but then he never did. "One day I might get the verdict in a fight I felt I'd lost," was his typical reaction – and that sporting behaviour was one of the reasons he became such an idol. Perhaps he also realised that by missing out on the welterweight title he was being allowed to grow naturally into the division where he was at his impeccable best – the middleweight. Trying to make weight while maturing can be a debilitating business.

It was at this stage that he met and married Blossom, the lady who was to become the single biggest influence on his life. He won the British middleweight title at 21 in 1929 and built up an impressive string of victories that led to a disastrous trip to New York and, almost unbelievably, three points defeats in a row. Ringside reports from spectators less biased than the judges indicated that in a city where aggression counts for more than it should, his opponents had scored many of their points by hitting his left fist with their faces. He cut short his contract and with Blossom's connivance returned home to another run of successes. He defended his middleweight title another four times – once outpointing Jack Casey over fifteen rounds only ten days after knocking out another opponent.

But no one disputes that 1933 was the most remarkable year of Harvey's career. He started it as British Middleweight Champion, lost that crown when he fought fifteen rounds one-handed against the great Jock McAvoy, yet finished up as Light Heavyweight *and* Heavyweight Champion, outpointing Jack Petersen. Against Petersen he used every trick learned from boyhood to tire the bigger, stronger, harder-hitting Welshman for the first five rounds, including holding on the blind side with what had been officially measured as the most powerful handgrip in the world. He was supposed to be able to exert a quarter of a ton of pressure. Then he boxed Petersen's head off to win clearly. And he did it

Harvey gets a kiss from his wife, Blossom, after a convincing win over his great rival Jock McAvoy.

Harvey starts to wake up and get up after the first knock-down by Mills, but is obviously dazed.

without earning a penny because without his knowledge Blossom, by then in charge of his affairs, had agreed with promoter Jeff Dickson to take the fight for expenses only. She was right. From then on every fight was for, in those days, big money. Len Harvey was a huge star in his own right, fêted wherever he went.

Unlike so many tragic others he was always aware that his fame depended on his skill and fitness. Until the war he boxed huge heavyweights, outpointing Larry Gains, the black Canadian, for the Empire title, drawing once with 15 stone Walter Neusel, the giant German. All his life his secret hero had been Bob Fitzsimmons, winner of three world titles, and although Harvey never quite touched those heights he won British titles at three weights, fought for world titles three times and won one version of the world light heavyweight title against his old rival Jock McAvoy.

When war broke out in 1939 he was British and Empire Champion at both light heavyweight and heavyweight and was privately plotting a world title fight against the great Joe Louis. He was, after all, in his own mind "only 32, fit, dedicated, experienced and immensely confident". Instead, three years later, ring-rusty, unfit, without the adequate preparation he always insisted upon, he went in against a fitter, stronger 22 year old who had been fighting regularly, and was knocked out for the first time in his life by another boxer who went on to achieve great things, Freddie Mills.

*Cameramen and ringside reporters are sent flying as Harvey falls out of the
ring. They helped him back in.*

FREDDIE MILLS
(1919 — 65)

During World War II the Royal Air Force took a day off to stage their own little battle on the ground on a Saturday afternoon in June 1942 at White Hart Lane soccer ground, home of Tottenham Hotspur. For a brief time a rather more important conflict in the skies was put aside, while a lowly aircraftman paid a corporal to strike a superior officer, with a sergeant the closest and most attentive witness. It was the day Corporal Freddie Mills knocked out Pilot Officer Len Harvey to become British and Empire Light Heavyweight Champion, with Sergeant Eugene Henderson as referee and Aircraftman John Muldoon the promoter.

To his own great credit Mills did not display much of the extrovert joy that was always a part of his charm, at the conquest of a man who had always been a personal hero, nor should he have done. Harvey, a prince of a man, was in his 35th year and had not fought for the past three of those. He was in no physical shape to meet an opponent who was a few days short of his 23rd birthday, and who obviously had a far more tolerant Commanding Officer. Mills had been fighting regularly during the early war years, including a couple of victories over the once fearsome but then fading Jock McAvoy. It was not much of a match against Harvey. Mills did have to spend the first round in a fruitless chase against a man who had mastered all boxing's elusive arts, but as soon as he landed a left hook early in the second the inevitable end had been signalled. Harvey was up at nine, but was swept back into the ropes by a barrage of punches, then knocked clean through them, out of the ring, banging his head on the floor as he went and failing to beat the count as he tried to climb back in.

That left hook was, for Freddie Mills, the most potent punch in a limited repertoire. He had quite a good left jab, but his right-hand punching was one of the crudest ever seen in a fighter who reached the top of his class. He threw it with an action strongly reminiscent of a fast bowler or, to pursue a wartime analogy, a grenade thrower, in a great whirling loop. It could be enormously effective when it landed, but few

Mills surprised Lesnevich with the quality of his boxing in their first fight, but the American avoided this jab and kept his crown.

opponents had trouble evading a blow they could see coming all the way from its inception around hip height and travelling in a huge unwieldy arc. It probably did real damage only in his learning days against the opponents he met as probably the last of England's champions to begin life in a travelling boxing booth as a teenager. He started boxing professionally at the age of sixteen, but seldom strayed far from his Bournemouth home, where in his early days he combined roadwork with his job as a milk roundsman.

He was an enormously popular attraction because of his crowd-pleasing all-action style and absolutely unquenchable spirit. Anyone who looked at his craggy, battered homely face with its cauliflower ear, busted nose and scarred eyes did not need to ask his profession. The victory over Harvey was in his 75th fight and after it the British Boxing Board of Control incidentally maintained a brave pretence that Mills was also World Champion at his weight. No one else agreed, particularly the Americans because they had more convincing claimants of their own in, first, Billy Conn, who almost beat Joe Louis and, later, the man who made Freddie Mills memorable, Gus Lesnevich. Before their own wars, however, there was another to finish. Mills served in India and the Far East and was still suffering from the after-effects of a malaria-type infection when he met the great Gus for the first time in May 1946.

Whenever people meet to argue about the most brutal, brave and ferocious championship fights of all times, this one comes into contention. Lesnevich set him up in the first round with jolting lefts and cracking rights for what looked like a certain finish in the second. Mills was down four times for long counts and in between he was drooping, hands down and defenceless as the punches pounded in to his unprotected head. The bell saved him from a knock-out.

Yet, in the third, Mills amazingly looked as strong as a bull again, actually taking the fight to the supremely confident Lesnevich and setting up a sequence of rounds, which even more astonishingly he dominated against a far better craftsmen with, of all things, an old-fashioned straight left. By the ninth round it was Lesnevich who looked in terrible shape. His nose was smashed, one eye was completely closed and cut.

Coming up in the tenth Mills revealed to his corner that he thought it was the third round – he had been fighting so bravely and boxing so brilliantly from instinct and memory. And it was during this round, in what must have been last-ditch desperation, that Lesnevich put all his own skill, strength and rhythm together again. Tremendous rights

A perfect example of Freddie's "Mills bomb", right, exploding this time on the side of Maxim's head.

dropped Mills for long counts and when it happened a third time, referee Eugene Henderson waved his arms in a signal that it was over – without starting a count. There were, in fact, only four seconds left of the round and inevitably his corner argued he could have recovered to carry on. Mills himself admitted, however, that he still suffered occasional headaches for the rest of his life after that fight, which makes the decision a correct one.

In the next two years Mills won and defended the European Light Heavyweight title, but he always had an unshakeable, though often badly dented, belief that he was strong enough to fight top-class heavyweights. Only three weeks after the Lesnevich epic, Ted Broadribb, a manager who should have known better, allowed him to take on British Heavyweight Champion Bruce Woodcock, who outclassed him over twelve hard rounds. Five months later a huge ranked American, Joe Baksi, several inches taller and 2 stone heavier, battered him in six rounds.

Yet in July 1948 Freddie Mills finally scaled his pinnacle and won the World Light Heavyweight Championship from Gus Lesnevich. The achievement was magnificent, sadly the performance less so. It was a dull, plodding, cautious affair with both probably remembering how dangerous the other had been the last time. Referee Teddy Waltham, later to become the British Boxing Board of Control secretary, actually had to call in the tenth round for more action – and that probably helped. Proud Freddie's stung response was to drop Lesnevich for two counts, clinching a points verdict. Britain had her first World Light Heavyweight Champion since Bob Fitzsimmons at the start of the century.

He still hankered after the heavyweights, however, particularly Bruce Woodcock, and there was surprise that he was not at ringside when the British Heavyweight Champion was in action one night. Freddie explained, "There had been a spate of burglaries round our way and I reckoned those who were doing it would think I was absent and the house unoccupied. So I sat waiting with the lights out. But they never came." Pity.

Woodcock beat him easily again in 1949, stopping him in the fourteenth round, and January 1950 saw his last brave fight in his 32nd year. Joey Maxim knocked out five of his teeth with vicious left jabs and knocked out the man himself in the tenth. But, like Henry Cooper in later years, Mills soared even higher in the respect and affection of the public after retirement. Amiable, likeable, amusing and articulate in a way that annoyed detractors of boxing, there are those who, to this day, refuse to believe that a man so full of life could have taken his own, as it is claimed, because of business worries. Freddie Mills always fought back.

CHRIS FINNEGAN
(1944 —   )

There may be the occasional purist who would query the nomination of Chris Finnegan as a great fighter. But no one can possibly dispute his right to be acclaimed as a great fighting man. He was a guy totally without fear of anyone inside or outside the ring and precious little respect either for anyone –with the possible exception of his vivacious wife Cheryl, always his most verbal and occasionally physical supporter at ringside.

Nor should anyone dispute his greatness as a character. He could not be subdued or overawed by anyone, something that was captured in one of the great anecdotes about him during the Mexico Olympics, when he won a gold medal at middleweight. During those games the Duke of Edinburgh addressed the British team and tried to encourage them to ignore the effects of the 7,000 feet altitude, recalling that he had played polo in Mexico and had noticed no effect from the lack of oxygen. Chris had the cockney nerve to put up his hand and ask HRH, "But 'ow did it affect the 'orses?" It brought the house down. Another indiscretion – staying out late in the Olympic Village - was, of course, conveniently forgotten when he came home with the only gold medal from the boxing team many thought he was fortunate to make. As ABA Champion two years earlier he had been bitterly disappointed not to be chosen for the trip to the Commonwealth Games in 1966 and in 1968 he had not even made the ABA finals.

It was at a pre-Olympic training session that the selectors started to realise that the uncouth, undisciplined Finnegan might even be an inspired choice. Medical tests proved that this 24-year-old unemployed bricklayer's labourer was far and away the fittest man in the squad, despite a lifelong affection for pints of Guinness. He had also engaged in literally hundreds of fights, some of them in pubs, most of them against other members of his own family, the Fighting Finnegans. To this day he swears the biggest hammering he ever had was at the age of twelve from his oldest brother, who was then 21.

Yet, as an amateur, Finnegan was definitely no rough-house brawler. Allied to the natural toughness that came from upbringing and the sort of strength he achieved running up ladders carrying a hundredweight of bricks was allied a southpaw jab, defensive ability and pure ambition. In his quarter-final he beat Mate Parlov, a Yugoslav, who later won the professional world light heavyweight crown. In the corridor of the boxing stadium they kept the rostrum that was dragged in for the medal ceremonies and every time Chris passed it he jumped on for a rehearsal. He did it for the last time when he beat Alexei Kiselyev in the final.

Then it was into the professional game under wise old Sam Burns as manager and the tough uncompromising Freddie Hill as trainer. Both knew that the southpaw style which won points in the amateur game would not attract punters in a harsher world. Chris had to adapt, take more chances, provide more aggressive action. He achieved it so successfully that by his fifteenth fight he was ready to train down from the light heavyweight he had become to tackle the reigning European Middleweight Champion, Tom Bogs, in Copenhagen in August 1970. It was called a draw, but Finnegan felt he narrowly won.

He was absolutely convinced he had won in a European light heavyweight title against a German, Conny Velensek, in Berlin the following year but again a draw was given and what Finnegan said could not be quoted in family newspapers the following day. Every fight fan

Some of Finnegan's sheer joy in the fun of fighting is captured in this training picture.

The trusty right hand that made Finnegan Olympic Champion missed this time, but the Russian has no target to attack.

who saw it on TV agreed, forcing a return fight in this country which Finnegan duly, inevitably, won easily. It was all warming up nicely for the biggest night of Chris Finnegan's life, a meeting with one of the truly great world champions, Bob Foster of Albuquerque, New Mexico. Foster was, quite rightly, a legend, a freakish 6 feet 3 inches tall. He had won the title four years earlier from Dick Tiger and defended it successfully more than a dozen times. The only two men who beat him during his reign were Muhammad Ali and Joe Frazier. Enough said.

Foster had knocked out Mike Quarry in Las Vegas in the fourth round. Chris saw the fight on closed-circuit television in London and reckoned that the left hook which finished the job was probably the hardest and finest single punch he had ever seen. But the one emotion Chris Finnegan never felt was fear. "I'll promise you this," he said. "Foster will have his share of bruises to count when he gets back home."

He kept that promise with impeccable tactics, staying out of trouble for most of the early rounds, then, as he reckoned some of the stamina was leaking out of Foster, who was in his 34th year, gradually increasing his own pressure. His willingness to slug it out almost cost him the fight in the tenth when a right had him down for eight, but the ferocity with which he fought back changed Foster's ideas of a summary finish and Chris was still there for the fourteenth, though trailing so far behind in points that victory was out of the question. He could have climbed on a bicycle and lasted out or gone for it. Typically Finnegan went for it and neither saw nor felt the left hook that knocked him out. But Foster said it all with his comment afterwards: "I hope someone else knocks him off because I sure don't ever want to have to fight him again."

It was back to the domestic scene – though hardly an anti-climax. John Conteh had emerged as a superbly talented 21-year-old winner of the European light heavyweight title. Chris still held British and Commonwealth crowns. Their first fight, a Wembley sell-out in 1973, was a war, with Chris always insisting that the blood which blinded him from the tenth round was from a butt, though he never disputed – nor should he – that Conteh had scored more points. It took a year to make a return fight, with Finnegan wickedly wise-cracking that Conteh needed all that time "to pickle his head and toughen it up". This was an unfortunate remark because it was undoubtedly a butt which split Finnegan's skull above his right ear, causing blood to start splashing so dramatically rather than merely flowing that the fight had to be stopped. Finnegan claims that given time to stop the blood he would have won.

But there were more fights and more controversy when both he and Johnny Frankham thought they had won a cracking fifteen rounder for the British title Conteh had vacated after winning the world title. Referee Harry Gibbs agreed with Frankham. But for the return four months later Finnegan was so fit and confident he even allowed his twelve-year-old daughter to see him dominate the return.

Chris was still dreaming, planning and intending to get back to the top at 32, when suddenly the curtain came down literally. A detached retina rendered him almost totally blind in his right eye. A great fighting man was forced to quit.

J O H N   C O N T E H
(1 9 5 1 —   )

Fighting for money at the highest level is not a game for squeamish cissies, nor for those who are just jolly good sports. That should dispose of the criticism most frequently levelled at John Conteh, a man who must figure prominently in every argument about the greatest English pound for pound fighter of the modern era. He caused grisly wounds around the eyes of many who fought against him and although that is its own tribute to the slashing precision of his fists, plenty have claimed he should have been made to wear an extra glove on his handsome head.

Before we all get too prissy about it, it should be remembered that some of the greatest world champions of all time were not noted for any regard for the rules – men such as Jack Dempsey, Rocky Marciano etc. Not that Conteh was ever a brawler. He was a scientist, a technician, an awkward man to handle both in and out of the ring. If he had not been quite so awkward about it, he might have had even more success than he achieved, which was still considerable. He spent too much of his time and, some feel, dissipated too much of his talent in disputes with promoters, managers and officialdom generally. Yet he always had a charismatic personality and a perfect physique, once summed up best by a pudgy sportswriter who sighed, "I'd love to borrow his body for a weekend. There are a couple of ladies I fancy and a couple of guys I detest". John cultivated his playboy image and sometimes lived up to it. At one stage his favourite poem could have been

> *My candle burns at both ends;*
> *It will not last the night;*
> *But, ah, my foes, and oh, my friends –*
> *It gives a lovely light.*

At the same time no fighter ever filled his frame with the fuel of pure fitness more assiduously than John Conteh when he was getting ready for action. He was destined for a great career when he won a Commonwealth gold medal as an amateur middleweight in 1970 at the

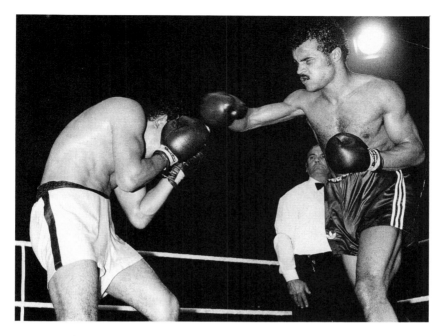

Conteh's expression captures all the determined aggression that helped him win the world title against Ahumada.

age of nineteen. He was a natural light heavyweight, but up among the big men was where the real money was and that was where Conteh always aimed to be. At the start of his career he regularly beat men up to 2 stone heavier, among them some useful performers. They included Billy Aird, who later boxed for the European title and Bill Drover, the Canadian champion who fought a draw with a young Joe Bugner. But this was the era when the world's top heavyweights were genuine Leviathans, huge hard men, and it became obvious that even at 6 feet tall and well proportioned, Conteh would never match the Alis, Fraziers and Foremans physically.

He almost immediately became European Champion, stopping a useful German Rudiger Schmidtke in twelve rounds to set up that fistic rarity – a natural by-public-demand meeting with the British and Commonwealth titles at stake also against popular Chris Finnegan. Conteh won bloodily on points but so narrowly that the promoters knew anyone who saw it would buy tickets for the return a year later. This time it was a cut – and arguably a butt – which settled it in Conteh's favour in six rounds, but Conteh's increasing natural strength was also a factor. Half a million Liverpudlians greeted his return to his home town riding on the top deck of an open bus – though even he might concede

*Conteh stayed comfortably and confidently ahead on points all through
his title defence against Alvaro Lopez.*

that the presence on that bus of Bill Shankly, the Liverpool football team
and two soccer trophies were contributory factors. It was around this
time, incidentally, that a rarely-glimpsed nice-guy side to Conteh was
seen when he took a fight for "peanuts" in his native Liverpool Stadium to
repay the fans who had followed him expensively in large
contingents.

By October 1974 he was more than ready for a shot at the world title
vacated by Bob Foster against Jorge Ahumada, an Argentinian with
impressive credentials. Four months earlier Ahumada had gone to
Foster's home town, Albuquerque, New Mexico, and emerged level on
points after fifteen rounds. Yet, against Conteh, Ahumada always came
second. At the end their faces told the story. Ahumada's left eye was cut
and closing. He looked as though he was wearing a headguard of bruises.
Conteh was virtually unmarked and up on his toes like a thoroughbred in
the winner's enclosure.

Then it all went sour. Just when he, as Champion, had the world at his
feet and a fortune within his grasp it was all snatched or taken away. In the
next three and a half years he had only four fights and had his title
stripped from him by the World Boxing Council. He spent only 99
minutes at the job he did best. There were more writs than right-handers.
To make it all the more frustrating, when he did fight he usually looked
brilliant. Five months after winning the title he defended it successfully –

*Anything goes! Ahumada comes boring in head first and Conteh wards
him off with an elbow on his way to victory.*

Finnegan was cut over the left eye in the return fight and was bleeding so profusely that it had to be stopped after six rounds.

and very ruthlessly - against an American, Lonnie Bennett. He cut his opponent's eye in the third and concentrated on the wound until it was stopped in the fifth. "Once the blood starts it is my job to keep it flowing," was his chilling comment afterwards.

There was a different chill in the atmosphere surrounding the relationship with his manager George Francis, who had always been a close friend. George was eventually to be demoted hurtfully to trainer on a smaller percentage of the prize-money that was no longer arriving regularly. Conteh became heavily involved in commercial commitments outside boxing – personal appearances, advertising and all the inevitable publicity a successful sportsman attracts. He was also busy squabbling with promoters, managers, the Board of Control, the world boxing authorities and, in a meaningless fight in America, broke his right hand in an overweight fight against an unknown Willie Taylor in August 1975.

It was another sixteen months, October 1976, before a Danish promoter came up with the sort of money he was demanding – £100,000 – to defend his title against a Mexican American, Alvaro Lopez, in Copenhagen. Astonishingly, Conteh's skill, speed and stamina all seemed undiminished as he won comfortably and unanimously on points. He defended the title once more, stopping another American, Len Hutchins, in three rounds in Liverpool before the WBC's patience snapped and they stripped him of his title.

He had to make a comeback when he should never have been away, but another chance was blown when, as a challenger, he never looked convincing in a fifteen-round fight against Mate Parlov of Yugoslavia in Belgrade – even though most British ringside observers thought he had won. He was 28 years old and a lot of years had been wasted before an uneasy armistice with promoters won him another lucky chance to regain the title from Matthew Saad Muhammad in Atlantic City in August 1979. Somewhere in all those years the very best of Conteh was lost. Yet he dredged up every reserve of skill to go close. He cut Saad Muhammad in the fifth in a clash of heads and was in front going into the thirteenth (so in today's era of twelve-round fights he would have been a winner again). But, knocked down twice in the fourteenth and battered throughout the rest of it, he had no complaints about the verdict. Saad Muhammad, however, had complaints in clusters about a decision ordering a re-match because illegal substances had been used to seal the gaping wound caused by Conteh's head, and made no mistake in the second fight seven months later. He waited three patient rounds to catch Conteh, then knocked him down and out in the fourth.

Shortly afterwards Conteh failed the British Board's strict medical examination and although he hotly disputed their verdict at the time, he should be grateful that he is now walking around healthy, witty and handsome. He should also be a great deal wealthier.

JOCK MCAVOY
(1908 — 71)

A fight against Jock McAvoy must have been a little like going to war against the Chinese Army. Punches never stopped coming at you from a man who seemed to feel a sort of primeval joy at the thrill of combat. No English fighter, at any weight, ever punched more devastatingly – and that is officially recognised. Statistics place McAvoy at the top of the records. Of his 133 victories in 147 fights he won 88 inside the distance and 53 of those opponents were knocked clean out. He hit like a heavyweight and, though never much more than a middleweight, fought in that division also.

As a member of a famous Manchester boxing stable which included World Flyweight Champion Jackie Brown and British Bantamweight Champion Johnny King, he had already stopped around 70 men when he had his first middleweight championship chance against Len Harvey, in March 1932, the first in a series of epic encounters. It was a complete contrast in styles because Harvey was a man of infinite patience, ice-cool, allowing all McAvoy's aggression to be countered by his own defensive mastery, then, in the fifth round, unleashing a right that lifted McAvoy through the ropes into the ringside seats. McAvoy landed on his head, but scrambled back, beat the count and started biting at the thumbs of his gloves. The Belle Vue crowd roared at a familiar warning sign – TV commentator Reg Gutteridge called it, memorably, "biting the hand that fed him". Some thought it was a sign of rage and frustration. Some thought it was an attempt to tear the padding inside the gloves to enable his knuckles to do more damage. It was, in fact, McAvoy's way of loosening joints that were already afflicted by arthritis.

He chased and harried and pounded at Harvey until the thirteenth round, and a terrible mistake. When Harvey dropped his arms in apparent exhaustion, McAvoy jumped, chin first, into another right so perfectly delivered that Harvey confessed afterwards he was astonished that it had not knocked McAvoy down, and out – "I thought it was hard enough to kill a horse." But at least it took enough of the steam out of

Jock for Harvey to keep his crown, though it was a close and controversial verdict. Both looked thoughtful afterwards – Harvey because he knew he would certainly have to go through it all again, McAvoy because he reckoned he realised where he had gone wrong.

Harvey always maintained that an injury to his right hand troubled him throughout their return fight in April 1933 in the same Belle Vue, Manchester, arena but certainly he never managed to land it as devastatingly when, this time, McAvoy was a clear points winner on non-stop aggression – and the new Middleweight Champion.

With Harvey moving up a weight, there were now virtually two middleweight divisions in Britain – one occupied by McAvoy, one by all the others. He held that title until relinquishing it voluntarily six years later in 1939, shortly before World War II, with one Lonsdale belt and two notches on another.

With any justice he would have become the first Englishman since Bob Fitzsimmons the previous century to win the World Middleweight title. He went to America in December 1935 where the reigning World Champion, Ed "Babe" Risko, insisted on protecting his crown with an overweight non-title fight. That showed excellent judgement. McAvoy had him down six times before the Babe went to sleep in 2 minutes and 48 seconds of the first round. What about the return fight? What return fight? Risko and his manager went suddenly deaf when McAvoy's name was mentioned. But New York fight fans were in love with McAvoy. He was their kind of guy, a very different sort of Englishman, though perhaps the name fooled them that he was Scots or Irish. It was not even his real name – he was born Joseph Bamford, but perhaps that did not have the right sort of ring.

They wanted him to stay on. He wanted to be world champion and, because he was never fussy about fighting bigger men, agreed to fight World Light Heavyweight Champion John Henry Lewis. By way of preparation he won two more tough fights in a total of twelve rounds, the second only a couple of weeks before the big one. It would never happen nowadays, partly because three months is accepted as the normal training time for a world title, partly because adequate medical supervision would have ruled McAvoy out. Both hands were badly bruised and swollen. It is a common fallacy among the non-cognoscenti that gloves were originally introduced to prevent the facial injuries bare knuckles could cause. The exact reverse is the truth. Gloves are there to protect the fists and McAvoy punched with such ferocity that the padding was not enough. His fists were so sore that they needed pain-killing injections before the fight in Madison Square Gardens on 13 March 1937. That might have helped, except that the Lewis dressing

*The size of the opponent never bothered Jock. This was the night he took on
Heavyweight Champion Jack Petersen.*

*It was the turn of very good lightweight Eddie Phillips to face Jock's
fighting fury and lose his British title.*

room heard about it and kept Jock waiting in the ring so that the effects wore off half-way through. McAvoy put up a good enough fight to be cheered all the way back to the dressing room – but they were cheers for a loser and the only consolation for McAvoy was that applause was not the usual reaction to a loser in front of a New York audience.

McAvoy admitted that he lost – rare in itself. He always felt there was something wrong if both men were still upright and conscious at the final bell. He was a genuine throwback to the bad old days when two went on until one dropped. He was advised by the doctors to rest for at least six months, yet not much more than *one* month later he was back in England challenging the *Heavyweight* Champion, Jack Petersen, with those same busted hands, losing on points inevitably. A year later, in April 1937, a brilliant Light Heavyweight Champion, Eddie Phillips, seemed to be boxing his way back into a fight which earlier had seen McAvoy swarm all over him. Then, in the fourteenth round, he walked into a cracking right and ten seconds later McAvoy had a second championship.

Jock always bitterly disputed the points verdict Len Harvey was awarded to take that Light Heavyweight title in April 1938 but it was, as usual, a memorable night with both in danger of inside-the-distance defeat at different stages and Harvey exhausted by body punches at the finish. Still, McAvoy had cause to be grateful to his shrewd, businesslike old rival. When John Henry Lewis was ruled out of a world title fight against Harvey after failing an eye test, the wily Len wrote to the Board of Control suggesting that, as the American was now effectively barred from the sport, another contest against McAvoy should be recognised for the vacant World Light Heavyweight Championship.

The Board agreed, and that guaranteed an 80,000 open air sell-out of the White City Stadium in July 1939. Pre-war critics who had been fortunate to see all four great fights, unhesitatingly plumped for this one as the most outstanding, with Harvey ahead on points for most of it, but desperately close to being stopped in the fourteenth. McAvoy was approaching the end. He fought occasionally for the few meagre purses available after war broke out and tried a brief comeback, at the age of 37, when it was over. There were three fights, with three more wins, but at the age of thirty it was obvious that the one man army had run out of ammunition.

A few years later McAvoy was crippled by polio, but even on crutches he could still be a warlike man – though you could say that he lost on points in one more unscheduled contest. Annoyed by something the well-known boxing author Gilbert Odd had written, he dropped his crutches to throw a left hook at the scribe, who devastated him by taking the blow calmly and said, "You've lost your punch, Jock."

RANDOLPH TURPIN
(1928 — 66)

Randolph Turpin's short, hectic and, in the end, desperately tragic life is captured perfectly in lines written by the eighteenth-century poet Thomas Mordaunt:

*One crowded hour of glorious life
Is worth an age without a name.*

Randy had his sixty minutes of genuine glory on the night of 10 July 1951 and England briefly became a better place to be when, over fifteen rounds, he outpointed Sugar Ray Robinson to become undisputed Middleweight Champion of the world.

That is no exaggeration. In those days when World War II was still fresh in unhappy memories, austerity, shortages and harsh times were part of everyday life for most people. Those lucky to be in a sold-out Earls Court, those who listened to a still-controversial radio broadcast – because it created the impression Robinson was winning easily – and those who read the ecstatic newspaper reports, walked around feeling a foot taller. To understand why, you have to understand the almost mystical awe with which Robinson was regarded – and rightly. There are many who continue to believe that he was the greatest pound for pound fighter of all time, of one hundred and thirty three previous fights he had lost just one, controversially to another great champion – Jake La Motta, the Raging Bull – a result he successfully avenged four times.

On a lightning tour of Europe Robinson had just beaten six useful men in six weeks, the most recently only nine days earlier in Italy. At thirty he was reckoned at the peak of his form. The betting boys in the huge arena would have had to pay out at odds of 20–1 against the points victory Turpin achieved – though even at those astronomical odds there were few takers. The realists all felt the 23-year-old Turpin had two chances – a dog's chance and no chance.

Perhaps they should all have studied more carefully Turpin's own background. The product of a mixed marriage between a West Indian

Turpin shows the muscular strength that enabled him to handle Robinson so easily in the clinches.

father who died when he was a schoolboy and a white mother, he had to fight constantly against what in those days was a racialist handicap. Seriously ill as a baby and deaf in one ear after being almost drowned as a twelve year old, he was blessed with two natural attributes – astonishing physical strength and the gift from God that is the prayer of all fighters, a natural one-punch knock-out power. As a seventeen year old he won both the ABA junior and senior titles and right from the start of his professional career as an eighteen year old he was an outstanding success against seasoned professionals. He stood 5 feet 10 inches with an unusually long reach. Purists felt that his stance was too unorthodox, with feet wide apart planted flat on the floor, yet it worked for Turpin. It gave him the leverage for punches that exploded when they landed. He did not lose until his twentieth fight – to the cagey and vastly more experienced Albert Finch, the man who was to take the British middleweight title from Randolph's older brother Dick Turpin (incidentally, the man who first broke British Boxing's disgraceful and shameful colour bar).

Randy stopped Finch in five rounds in a return match in October 1950 and added the European title four months later by another one-punch KO of a Dutchman, Luc Van Dam, in a contest that lasted precisely 48 seconds, including the count. Turpin was not exactly a novice when he stepped in against Robinson. It was his 44th professional fight.

In all truth the Robinson fight was never the classic it has sometimes been portrayed – for the simple, if startling, reason that Randolph dominated most of it, particularly after Robinson's left eye was cut in the seventh round. It is true that Robinson almost certainly underestimated him. It is also true that during his Continental "working holiday" the American marvel had neither lived nor behaved like a monk. "He had too much Paris in his legs," was how one US scribe summed up cynically. It is also true that he never successfully found his way past a Turpin left jab that was a real punch not just a probing prod. Nor could he get inside, for Turpin's natural strength held and turned and shoved him around.

Turpin's "crowded hour of glorious life" that made him World Champion was to last just 64 days. He lost the return to Robinson in a tenth round of what had until then been a fairly even fight, and as there were no doubts about Robinson's fitness this time this emphasises how good Turpin really was. Then the American, the challenger, had his eyebrow split after a mid-ring collision. He must have doubted whether he could fight five more rounds with a wound so wide and deep, so dredged up everything he had learned in his whole fighting life and threw it all at Turpin. The Englishman was down for nine from a vicious right and was then driven back on to the ropes by a blur of blows. The middle rope supported his sagging frame and Robinson landed a whole series of punches to an unprotected head until the referee stopped it with only eight seconds remaining of the round.

If Turpin had taken another couple of counts he might, with a minute's rest, have been able with his enormous stamina to recover. But a film of that finish, studied half a dozen times, made referee Ruby Goldstein's decision to stop the fight a humane and justifiable one. It is also true that Turpin was never quite as good again – though there were extraneous other reasons why. His marriage failed. He was caught up in an alleged assault case brought by an American showgirl. He started to have his tax troubles.

However, he remained a significant figure in his own backyard, which included the whole of Europe. He won the British light heavyweight title from a weight-weakened Don Cockell, moved down again to capture the Empire and European titles at middleweight and qualified for another shot at the world middleweight title, disgracefully declared vacant even though Sugar Ray Robinson still dominated the division. The opponent was the undistinguished Carl Bobo Olsen, a Swedish-American Turpin should have destroyed. Instead he skimped his preparation, outboxed Olsen for only three rounds and then performed so far below par that his brother Dick left his corner in disgust. The points defeat verdict was unanimous and the rest was

Note the unusually wide-apart position of Turpin's feet. It added power to his punches – though this left missed.

virtually a plunge downhill. Tiberio Mitri knocked him out in a round to take the European title, an undistinguished Gordon Wallace knocked him out in four rounds; although he managed three successful defences of his British title, he was the shell of a once great fighter when Yolande Pompey knocked him out in two rounds in September 1958.

Business ventures went disastrously wrong. The Inland Revenue men were hounding him. He even indulged in professional wrestling after an abortive comeback three years into what should have been a fur-lined retirement. Turpin committed suicide aged 37 in 1966.

TERRY DOWNES
(1936 —   )

There was always something distinctly different about Terry Downes, the rumbustious Paddington middleweight who was to become World Champion at his weight and came heartbreakingly close in a higher division. It was obvious from his first professional appearance in London aged twenty. He did not duck through the ropes shyly. He jumped over them and immediately pranced round the ring whirling both arms like windmills and indulged in some colourful calisthenics in his corner. He did not wait to attract attention. He demanded it.

His background was equally colourful. He had spent his teenage years in America, three of them in the Marine Corps for whom as a Services champion he boxed more than fifty times, so successfully that he was selected for the USA Olympic team in Melbourne – until they discovered he was British. He became an immediate big attraction even after a disastrous one-sided defeat in only his third pro fight in five rounds at Shoreditch Town Hall, by a then unknown Nigerian called Dick Tiger, later Middleweight and Light Heavyweight World Champion, when panic-stricken bookmakers who had made Terry 7-1 favourite tried frantically to hedge their bets as he was bounced up and down like a yo-yo before being badly cut. This was also the start of his reputation for memorable one-liners because, when asked afterwards who he might meet next, he said, "I'd like it to be the bastard who suggested Dick Tiger". A similar occasion occurred on a Sports Forum in Wormwood Scrubs when some of the convict inmates were heckling him. They fell about when he warned, "Careful or I'll take you outside".

Downes perfected his own style of storming, swarming non-stop attacks that sickened and disheartened as much as they hurt. It was the style he had learned in the States, but he never forgot the basics he had been taught in more orthodox amateur days with the famous Fisher club in London. That was to be amply demonstrated in the fight that first pushed him into the world rankings. He was British Middleweight Champion in his twentieth fight against Welshman Phil Edwards, losing it briefly to a Scot, John "Cowboy" McCormack, on a disqualification, but regaining it decisively in eight rounds. Now, in October 1960, in an official world title eliminator he was up against Joey Giardello, officially rated number three and hailed in New York and Philadelphia, where they know about such things as the complete boxer-fighter.

The way Downes handled his opponent was masterly. When Giardello tried to box, Downes fought him. When Giardello tried to fight back, Downes boxed him off with stiff, spearing left jabs from a copybook few realised Terry had even read. Giardello who had won well over a hundred fights was completely dominated. Those who had first written off Downes' chances, and then claimed that at thirty Giardello was over the hill, were rebuked three years later when the American won the middleweight crown from a certain Dick Tiger. Downes was fully entitled to engage in one of his more mischievous pursuits – parading around the ring afterwards, singling out boxing writers who had forecast failure for him and leaning across the ropes to criticise their judgement, and sometimes their parentage.

He was also fully entitled to the world championship shot he won against Paul Pender of Boston, a man who is still inclined to be underrated as a champion even though he twice beat Sugar Ray Robinson to win and retain his crown. Downes, forgetting the Giardello lesson, kept walking forward against a defensive master of retreat and smother tactics with a cutting, counter-attacking style. Knocked down in the first round and punished steadily, the fight was eventually stopped in the seventh with blood everywhere, all of it Terry's. For Pender it

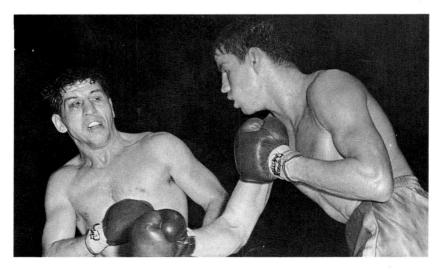

The night Downes outboxed a boxer. Joey Giardello is already showing signs of damage against unmarked Terry.

Downes was always a more thoughtful boxer and a better strategist than most believed. This catches him in pensive mood.

certainly seemed an easy enough job for him to be tempted into a return fight in London, though he still took the precaution of having Terry's comparatively meagre £7,000 purse frozen in a Boston bank to ensure a third match if it became necessary – as it did.

In the return fight, staged incidentally exactly one day after the tenth anniversary of Randolph Turpin's victory over Robinson, Britain had a world champion again, but in astonishingly anti-climactic circumstances. In the nine rounds it lasted, neither achieved much ascendancy, though in that ninth Pender looked a class in front, punished Downes clinically, won the round convincingly and then retired on his stool. He had been cut, but not seriously, and there was even ridiculous talk of a betting coup. The more likely truth is that Pender, realising how strong Downes still was, put everything he had left into that round, discovered it was not enough and had little of anything, including heart, for the six more hard rounds he faced. Certainly Downes, although proud of his title, felt Pender had robbed him of some of the glory that was his due. Seven months later Downes had to go back to Pender's home town where the bank still held his money and there he lost a narrow but

*Downnes's famous "bleedin' hooter" and both eyes came in for so much
punishment that Pender won their first fight in seven rounds.*

unanimous points verdict on a night when a local referee allowed the crowd's favourite son to get away with so much grabbing and holding it infuriated Downes - and prompted thoughts of retirement.

Wise investments, prompted by his marvellously protective manager, Sam Burns, made him a rich man with all the trappings - a Mill Hill mansion, a Rolls Royce, public school education booked for his children - but Downes still had driving ambition and a genuine love for the game. He had seven winning fights in a row including one over Sugar Ray Robinson - his own, and many other people's great hero - though to his credit he never claimed it gave him much pleasure. "Harry Levene couldn't have paid me enough to take him on at his best," he said afterwards.

There was one more great night at Belle Vue, Manchester, in November 1960 with Downes, by then a light heavyweight, taking on, against all the odds, the American Willie Pastrano, who had a couple of years earlier been too smart a boxer for some of Britain's best heavyweights - Brian London, Dick Richardson, Joe Bygraves. Technically vastly superior, Pastrano was completely shaken out of his normal elegant rhythm by the controlled fury of Terry's attacks.

By the eleventh the American was trailing, dejected, disheartened and tiring against a challenger full of cockney confidence. Then his manager, Angelo Dundee, produced a master stroke - or rather two. As Pastrano came unwillingly off his stool Dundee smacked him hard twice, stingingly, insultingly, two open-handed full-blooded whacks on the behind. Pastrano turned on him angrily and Dundee snarled, "Don't hit me, hit HIM" - pointing at Downes. Pastrano exploded a right to the head and Terry was down. Up at eight he was caught and hurt by another flurry of fury and was on his way down when Andrew Smythe, Britain's most respected referee of the time, stopped it with Downes on his way to the floor.

Downes, in tears afterwards - not the blubbering of self-pity but in rage and frustration - claimed that he was merely seeking a breather, that given it he could have gone on, would have won. But it did not look that way to many of us in the place. He retired immediately but, unlike so many who became rich and famous, he never turned away from the sport. You can still see him at almost every show - and if he is there you will certainly hear him providing roaring, raucous encouragement to the performers. It is possible he still envies them.

World Champion at last. Downes holds aloft the trophy awarded after he had forced Pender to retire.

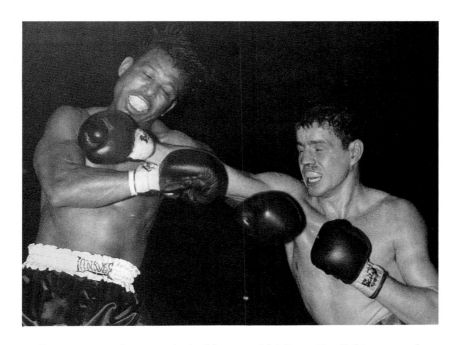

Downes meets the man who had been an idol, Sugar Ray Robinson, and outpoints the old warrior convincingly.

JOHNNY PRITCHETT
(1943 —   )

There are still those boxing enthusiasts who look at Johnny Pritchett's record when he decided to retire five days after his 26th birthday, the undefeated British Middleweight Champion, and an athlete at the peak of his physical powers – and wonder whether it was a wicked waste of considerable natural talent. Pritchett had, arguably, the best success percentage of any English fighter in boxing history. In 34 fights, only once did a referee lift an opponent's arm in victory. It happened in Milan in February 1969.

Johnny was challenging for the European Middleweight title against the home-town hero, a useful enough fighter called Carlos Duran. He outboxed, outmanoevred and outclassed his man through most of it and by the thirteenth round seemed to be coasting as comfortably downhill to victory as an errand boy with feet up on the handlebars of a bicycle. Then that referee, without any previous warnings, disqualified Pritchett for a butt that no one else had noticed. Even the partisan Italian crowd whistled and howled their protests at the blatant injustice and every Italian newspaper, next day, condemned it.

Pritchett immediately retired, but has always maintained that it was not in anger, disgust or disillusion, rather a calculated, logical decision he has never regretted. Many years later he said, "The referee's decision was so daft it was unbelievable. The only butting done was by Duran's head against my gloves. But I wasn't getting really big money. My purse for that one was only £3,000. I was starting to have to work hard to make the middleweight limit. My painting and decorating business was starting to make money and I was too short to grow into a successful light heavyweight." It seemed to him logical to call it a day.

Those who look at him now, cannot deny that Pritchett always knew what he was doing. He owns up cheerfully to being a millionaire, owner of a metalwork company that employs 50 well-paid people. He is one of the many ex-fighters riding around in large cars and making big decisions, defying the image the anti-boxing brigade like to portray as

Pritchett was at his peak the night he outclassed a tough Jamaican, Milo Calhoun, to win the Commonwealth title.

the more usual fate of boxers – that of pathetic, exploited has-beens, shambling through life seeking handouts. There are several more contemporary millionaires who could tell such people differently – with the obvious "for instances" of Terry Downes, Dave Charnley and Henry Cooper – but Pritchett is different again from these ex-boxers in that his ring earnings did not match theirs. The foundation of his fortune was the £3,000 from that final fight, ploughed initially into his first business and the profits from it enabling him, in the early seventies, to diversify so successfully.

But even though Johnny Pritchett himself has no regrets, there are those who have. When he quit, the Middleweight Champion of the world was a distinctly useful Italian, Nino Benvenuti, but Pritchett had a competence that must have given him an outside chance of the top crown. He had, in fact, shown some of his own abilities against another world champion at least as good as Benvenuti, Terry Downes – though admittedly only in the gymnasium.

When Downes was preparing for his 1964 world title challenge against Willie Pastrano, Pritchett sparred regularly with the cockney challenger, hit that rumbustious character with more left jabs than Pastrano ever managed and regularly boxed rings round him. Gymnasium form is, of course, notoriously unreliable, but Downes himself paid Pritchett some typically ungrudging compliments – "That kid is gonna give some poor bleeder all the bruises they can count."

At that time, Pritchett, twice an ABA champion and silver medallist in the Commonwealth Games in Australia in 1962, had been a professional for about a year, with Alan Rudkin and Frankie Taylor, in the bright young stable run by Bobby Neill. He built up a steady run of professional victories with a neat, complete armoury of intelligent boxing, a good defence and occasionally hurtful punching. He got his championship chance early, against an old pal, Wally Swift, who may have thought he was doing the ambitious 22 year old a favour with a voluntary defence of his title in his native Nottingham in November 1965. Swift had sparred with the young Pritchett, then an amateur, while he was building his own career. At 29 he was vastly more experienced, a thoroughly seasoned professional for nine years and a former British and Empire Welterweight Champion. It was even thought that he saw the fight as a quick chance for the first notch on the Middleweight Lonsdale belt he had just won.

It was not quite like that. In fact it was not a bit like that. Pritchett was ahead on points when the fight was stopped in the twelfth by Harry Gibbs, with Swift, unable to see out of a damaged left eye, drifting further behind on points and, in his condition, liable to get seriously hurt. Any arguments about it were comprehensively settled when Pritchett was a clear points winner of the return, in February 1967, by the equivalent of three rounds on the scorecard of the referee, the late Wally Thom, a man who knew the business as a former British, Commonwealth and European Welterweight Champion. Within a week of his 24th birthday Pritchett had won a Lonsdale belt of his own, outright, for in between the Swift fights he had battered the tough Mancunian, Nat Jacobs, to defeat in eleven rounds in Manchester.

He mopped up the British challengers with a clear points win over the Liverpudlian, Les McAteer, who was to win the title when Pritchett quit. But most good judges would agree that he was at his absolute peak in a return fight, with the Commonwealth title on the line, against a slippery, skilful and very tough Jamaican, Milo Calhoun, who had achieved the only draw on Pritchett's record. The Jamaican, who had never been stopped inside the distance in more than 40 fights, against some of the best around, was managed by George Gainford, not a man to concern himself with nonentities – he had also managed Sugar Ray Robinson through all that marvellous man's greatest days – and not known either for a soft-hearted, merciful attitude. Yet Gainford pulled Calhoun out of it after eight rounds of cold, controlled ferocity by Pritchett at Belle Vue, Manchester, in October 1967. Afterwards, the Jamaican, with blood leaking from his nose and mouth, both eyes closing, his chest heaving, legs trembling, sweat-soaked and exhausted, reached for the microphone and announced to the crowd: "Pritchett is a great fighter. You have a future world champion."

That was never to be. Pritchett went on steadily winning and improving, however, until that shock "defeat" by Duran and his retirement, to the business that blossomed in the seventies to make him wealthy. He still laughs when he recalls that some people thought he might not be a sufficiently quick thinker for the harsh world of commerce. He still says, "I never wanted to think quickly and perhaps make mistakes. I always wanted to think slowly and definitely make money." He is a great advertisement for the game.

Pritchett's career was short, but he still managed to win two Lonsdale belts –
though he does not need the £1 a week pension.

ALAN MINTER
(1 9 5 1 —   )

Alan Minter dropped his guard – metaphorically speaking – during a very memorable interview. The answer to a question about what he wanted most from a boxing career that was just beginning to blossom, was different from the usual. "Memories," he said. "The sort of memories I can tell to my kids and the kids they will have. When they ask me what grandad did for a living I'll be able to tell them I was a good fighter at my own weight, because I am. But if I win the World Middleweight title I'll be able to tell them that I was the best. Won't that be something?" The eyes of a fighting man softened briefly.

Minter, of course, achieved that towering ambition but there was a time in his career when it seemed so remote that it was almost out of sight. After winning a bronze medal at the Munich Olympics as a 21 year old in 1972 – he still insists that only disgraceful political judging robbed him against a German in the semi-finals – he turned professional. They nicknamed him "Boom Boom" Minter for the emphatic grunts that accompanied his jolting southpaw jab.

Frankly he did not really start to fight like a professional until he had been in the game another three years. That was directly due to a distinctly amateurish fault. Whenever he was caught and hurt, which is inevitable in his game, his immediate instinct was wild uncontrolled retaliation. He would go flailing in, head down and careless, which is why he suffered a series of eye injuries and occasional defeats by lesser fighters. But at least it was a fault in the right place – the heart of the man – and it was one worked on constantly by the man who became his trainer, one of boxing's best teachers, Bobby Neill. He added better balance and control by 1975, the year Alan outpointed Kevin Finnegan to become British Middleweight Champion.

It was a fifteen-round "war" and so was the return which Minter also narrowly won a year later, because not only was Finnegan a considerable opponent in his own right, courageous and skilful, Minter discovered that his southpaw style for once held no hidden mysteries.

Finnegan had probably boxed and sparred more rounds against a right-fist-first fighter than anyone else in the country, most of them against his famous older brother Chris.

It was in that same year Minter showed signs of making the quantum leap into world class, particularly in the month that ended it. He signed for a December fight against the highly ranked "Sugar Ray" Seales, the North American Champion, reckoned to be the next in line for a crack at the then World Champion, the menacing Carlos Monzon. Minter put a stop to that little dream after taking a genuine dislike to the American's pre-fight threats – "I'm going to rough up, mess up, cut up Minter. He is in trouble". Minter said, "That sort of rubbish gets right up my nose. I've never been hurt by hard words or dirty looks. They are going to have to pick him up when it's over." He threw the best right hand punch of his career to drop Seales in the fifth round and went on battering him until the fight was stopped.

He threw a left hook in the same class to win the European championship against an Italian, Germano Valsecchi, in Milan two months later. Valsecchi was moving forward at the time, the fifth round, doubling the impact and was so completely concussed the referee could have counted to thirty. "I have never been hit and hurt so much in my life," he said when he woke up. The fight was also notable for being the first European championship to be won in that city by an Englishman.

Minter did an impressive demolition job cutting and battering Vito Antuofermo to keep his world title.

But that year, 1977, which Minter hoped would see him soar up the ratings was to turn sour. Cuts cost him his European title against the tough Marseilles fighter, Gratien Tonna, and an expensive defeat by a very talented American, Ronnie Harris. He had also been stripped of his British title because of his European commitments. It was back in the capable hands of Kevin Finnegan and Minter had to endure another fifteen rounds to retrieve it. He had to return to Italy to regain his European title from another Italian, Angelo Jacopucci, an occasion darkened by tragedy. Jacopucci, knocked unconscious in the twelfth round by a left hook, was later taken to hospital where he died. Alan's reaction when he was wakened by his then manager and father-in-law, Doug Bidwell, was a dazed disbelief. After the fight he had praised Jacopucci saying, "They told me the guy wasn't game. Well I hope I don't ever have to fight anyone braver." Later at a reception the two men talked and laughed together – boxing has always been that sort of sport. Minter went out alone in a rowing boat to think it all over – ironically it had been earlier during that same trip he had talked so longingly about his world title dreams – and decided he had to carry on. Two undefeated years later the dream came true.

Vito Antuofermo was the only undisputed Champion of the world at that time – the two warring World authorities, the WBA and the WBC each had a different man ruling all the other divisions. He had already boxed a draw with Marvin Hagler and, although a controversial verdict, it was its own testimony to his toughness. He had a jaw of steel and a heart as big as a cabbage. His "style", if you could call it that, was to walk through everything thrown at him and sicken the other man with his strength. It was a method that suited Minter, who survived one scare when a sparring partner grazed him over the left eye. "I've had worse cuts shaving," snapped Minter. "I've waited too long for this one to risk a postponement. Let's get it on."

It was tough, gruelling, desperately close. Minter constantly caught Antuofermo with good solid southpaw jabs, but then hitting this man was never a problem. Hurting him was a different matter as he too kept coming forward, scoring his own points by sheer persistence. The American judge gave the fight to the Englishman by two points. A Venezuelan decided Antuofermo had done it by the same margin. The English judge appalled the whole of the American boxing fraternity and most of the British by making Minter the winner by *twelve* clear points. He gave Antuofermo only one round, the fourteenth, when Minter was knocked down for the first time in his career.

Minter did a far more convincing job in the return fight in London when he stopped Antuofermo in eight completely one-sided rounds. "I

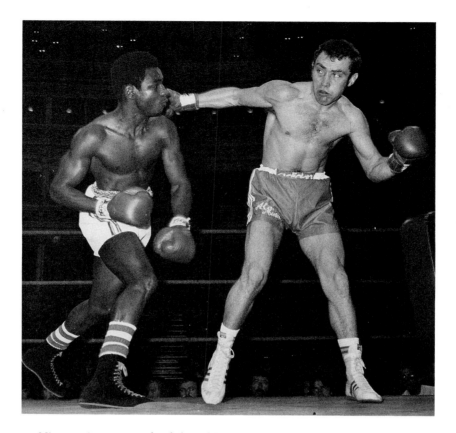

Minter misses a man he did not like, Ray Seales, with a jab from the right, but is ready to let the left fist go.

watched the film of the first fight a hundred times," said Minter afterwards, "and I knew I had to stand my ground, put my punches together. I knew if I did that and started faster I could bust him up." He was right.

It is history now that three months later he made the mistake of trying to take the fight to a master boxer, one of the all-time greats, Marvin Hagler, and was so severely punished for it by clinical cutting punches that it had to be stopped in the third round for Minter's face to be pulled together again with stitches. At thirty it was time for Minter to move over for a younger man, and Tony Sibson removed him from the scene, replacing him as European Champion in three rounds.

TONY SIBSON
(1958 —   )

Sam Burns, one of the wisest, craftiest, hardest and best of all boxing managers, used to tell an interesting story about how and why he signed, and then steered to a world middleweight title and a financial fortune, the fighting gypsy, Tony Sibson. It happened just after one of Sam's own stable, the clever, immensely brave, Kevin Finnegan had outpointed that same Sibson to regain the British Middleweight title in 1979. Sam, in that famous, slow, sleepy, cockney drawl said, "Kevin kept on pestering the life out of me about how this kid he beat could take your face off with a jab, bust your ribs with body shots and keep on walking through anything you threw at him. I thought what the hell, maybe I can do something with him. Kevin was 31 and nearly finished. This kid was only 21."

No one really knows how far Tony Sibson might have gone if he had achieved his full potential. He had genuine Romany blood in him which could see his mood veer between elation and deflation, provide days when he could lick the world and times when he did not feel like getting out of bed. He was difficult to discipline because he could not discipline himself. But there was genuine talent there and it broke out often enough to make him worth watching. He had a real fighter's physique, skinny but strong legs, and, from the waist up he was built like a circus strong man with wide sloping shoulders, a deep chest, thick neck and forearms, and big biceps. There was a punch to match, a left hook.

He came from Leicester and had almost all his first 30 fights in the Midlands, attracting a growing army which followed him devotedly throughout his career. Exactly one day after his 21st birthday, on 10 April 1979, he won the British Middleweight title against Frankie Lucas, a tough flashy favourite who annoyed Sibson so much with Muhammad Ali style gibbering, scowling and threatening that Sibson tried to throw punches before the start. He went on throwing them, knocking Lucas down three times in the fifth before the fight was stopped.

Tony always reckoned he had been kidded out of his title by the wily Finnegan in November the same year, fooled into failing to go for a quick finish when he had a man, ten years older and more experienced, shaken. He intended to prove that in December 1980 when he went in against a tough southpaw from Italy, Matteo Salvemini, who had taken the European title fight from Finnegan. Sibson won six rounds in a row at the Albert Hall and then battered the Italian with a flurry of head punches for a knock-out win. For Sam Burns it was time to find out about Tony Sibson's chances in a higher class. "A manager can protect his fighter too much. He can also drop him in it too soon. I think I know the difference," said Sam. He pitched Sibson in against an Argentinian, Norberto Cabrera, who had never been knocked down by the three world champions he had fought.

It looked a dangerous mistake when Sibson was knocked down by a cracking right in the first round, in January 1981, but that was the only one of the ten rounds he lost. He had arrived, and was to prove it in sensational style against ex-World Champion Alan Minter, on a night in September 1981 that sold out Wembley. Sibson was superb, dropping Minter with savage hooks, breaking his nose, cutting him and stopping him inside three rounds of a merciless beating. "I respected Minter but he had been to the top. He couldn't have been as hungry for success as I was," said Tony. "When my career is over I don't want to finish up clocking on at a factory. I want a big house with a couple of acres and some nice horses."

Sibson had grown into British boxing's main hope at the end of an era which had seen a succession of world champions – light heavyweight Conteh, middleweight Minter, light middleweight Maurice Hope, welterweight John Stracey, and lightweight Jim Watt. All the kings had gone. Promoter Micky Duff saw Sibson as a man who might make millions, but the typical Romany rejoinder was, "I wonder if Micky would lend me a hundred grand now on the strength of all the money he says I could make one day."

Privately, Sam Burns was already becoming irritated at Tony's occasional reluctance to give up the good things of life for the fortune he felt was there for the taking by a really dedicated fighter – though Sibson did get himself impressively fit for the most important one so far in his career. In February 1982, in Birmingham's National Exhibition Centre, he was matched in an official world championship eliminator against a top-rated American, Dwight Davison, four inches taller than Sibson's 5 feet 8 inches and a superb boxer. "I've fought tall men before," said Sibson. "You fold them over with body punches, then you hit them in the head. It's simple."

The judges obviously agreed with him. One of them did not give Davison a round in a close, tough fight, which was ridiculous because,

Tony Sibson put everything into his make or break victory over Argentinian Norberto Cabrera, winning nine of the ten rounds.

apart from anything else, it created the impression of an easy job and robbed Sibson of some of the credit for the boxing intelligence and driving determination of a victory over a man he praised extravagantly: "I don't believe there is a stronger, more awkward middleweight in the world," he said. But there was.

Everything about Tony Sibson's challenge for Marvin Hagler's World Middleweight title in Worcester, Massachusetts, in February 1983 was wrong, including his preparation. He did no sparring, only roadwork and punching the heavy bag in the gymnasium, scandalising one visitor, former Middleweight Champion, Terry Downes. "That don't mean a bleeding thing," Downes scoffed. "The bag ain't got arms to block punches or fists to whack you one back. You can't get sharp without sparring partners. I've never known anything like it from someone who wants to be a world champion." Still, like everyone else, he gave Sibson "a puncher's chance". The trouble was, Sibson was never given a chance to land even one effective punch. The brooding, scowling Hagler gave

Sibson a humbling lesson. Wherever Tony tried to put his head, Hagler found it, with cutting, ripping, hurting blows that stopped him in six rounds. The only good thing that seemed to come out of it was Sibson's repentant attitude afterwards. It briefly promised to see him re-born with a new attitude of determination to come back and learn the game all over again. It was almost touching to see him approach Hagler, humble and subservient as any autograph hunter, at the post-fight party the following night. "Thank you. You made me a man. You taught me what I have to do to become a champion like you." At his own press conference he promised English sportswriters, one of whom had actually been naïve enough to tip him, "I'm going to tell my manager I want to be taken out of cotton wool, thrown to the wolves, made to fight for my life against dangerous men. Money doesn't matter. This big pay day will finance my boxing future. It will be spent getting me ready, paying for top class sparring and fighting."

Sibson was only 24. It sounded encouraging. He could still, as he said, "get out of bed in the morning and lick any middleweight in Europe" – something his career proved. He had seven European title fights and won them all. He even, briefly, kept his word. He trained for three weeks in a tough Florida gymnasium, having wars every day with sparring partners who knew the business, before his next job in America, a two-rounds demolition in Atlantic City of "Irish" John Collins, a Bostonian who had been touted as future championship material before Tony went to work on him.

But the dedication did not last. He again travelled to the States, three weeks before a January 1984 fight against Don Lee in Atlantic City, but this time took his lady, Julie, and their eight-month-old baby son, because having them around for Christmas and New Year made him feel contented. Contented is the last thing a fighter should feel and Lee cut him up badly, beating him in eight rounds.

There were long gaps between fights now that he was wealthy, owned the big house, the field and the horses. He took the whole of 1985 off and , although under the new management of Frank Warren there were two more world title fights, they brought only two more disappointments. He stepped up a weight to challenge Dennis Andries in September 1986 for the WBC Light Heavyweight Championship and was sharply reminded of a boxing truth – "the bigger they are, the harder they hit you". It was stopped in nine rounds. In his last fight in February 1988, and still only 29, he was comprehensively outboxed by American Olympic gold medallist, Frank Tate, for the IBF version of the Middleweight title and knocked out in the tenth. We never did learn how good Tony might have been.

MAURICE "MO" HOPE
(1951 —   )

The light middleweight division could have been invented and designed to fit Maurice "Mo" Hope as perfectly as the impeccable bespoke tailored suits he favoured towards the end of his career. The World Light Middleweight Championship crown sat just as snugly on a head which could have modelled for a noble bronze bust. He had travelled a long way on a journey from a shack in his native Antigua to a house in North London that ranked in the mansion class.

So, why talk of Maurice Hope as English? Because, quite simply, that was how Mo saw himself. After he won the world title from an Italian in Italy he said, "My dream is to defend it in England because that is where I feel unbeatable. England is my home, the place where I belong, the country that made me." Technically he could have become a tax exile because in recognition of his achievement the Antiguan Government deeded him two acres of their attractive West Indian island. As a property owner he was entitled to bank his money there, but he rejected the idea. The cost of British citizenship, to a man in the tax bracket to which he aspired, was prohibitive but he was prepared to pay it. It would have been un-English not to.

Still, that is racing ahead of a story through which runs a thread of spitting defiantly in the face of adversity – with only very occasional better breaks. The first of these came in 1973, when, much later than they should have done, the British Boxing Board of Control finally recognised and introduced an official light middleweight division at 11 stone. Mo Hope won it the following year and remained the best in Europe by a distance for another eight years until his retirement. Without it he would still have been extremely useful but could never have achieved greatness.

He would have found it impossible to get down to the welterweight limit of 10 stone 7lbs and the real middleweights, the 11 stone 6lbs men, were just too big for him. Mo Hope found that out the hard way when, in June 1975, he made his challenge for the British Middleweight title, held by the very useful and much larger Bunny Sterling, who occasionally came in at more than 12 stone for overweight fights. The turning point came in the seventh, when Hope let go and landed with his own best punch – a left hook, perfectly timed, perfectly delivered to the head – and absolutely nothing happened. A man you cannot hurt is someone you cannot beat and Mo was stopped in the next round.

Against men of his own size it was distinctly different. He won his European title the following year when he went to Rome and cut to pieces Vito Antuofermo, good enough later to become undisputed World Middleweight Champion. The Italian had to take two standing counts before the referee stopped the fight in the fifteenth. Hope himself always believed he won the World Light Middleweight title in Berlin in March 1977 but it was called a draw and the lanky German Eckhardt Dagge kept the title – to his own great surprise. The British judge Harry Gibbs who made Hope the winner by three clear rounds scored it just about right and Dagge, to his credit, came over to Hope at the end and said, "Sorry, but I don't make the decisions". Hope himself was almost incoherent in his distress for just about the first time in his life.

Mo, an intelligent and articulate man, was a warm and kind character outside the ring. All his impressive skilful aggression disappeared when he pulled the gloves off – "I don't have to hate a man to hurt him," he said. His prayers for a quick return were not answered. Dagge lost the world title to a tough Italian-Australian, Rocky Mattioli, who came from the same Italian village from which the parents of one Francis

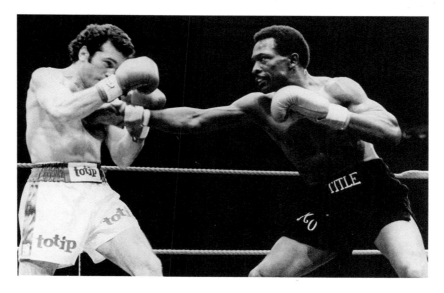

That southpaw right jab of Hope's, stabs through Mattioli's guard and the left hook is cocked and ready.

Marcheggiano, better known later as Rocky Marciano, had emigrated.

Mattioli, built like a miniature Marciano, was in no great hurry to meet Hope and the British Boxing Board actually threatened to resign from the World Boxing Council if that body failed to order a match. The chance finally arrived in March 1979, a full two years after he felt he had won it. Hope himself was surprisingly philosophical as he travelled to San Remo, Italy, for the fight: "Maybe I didn't want to win the title then as much as I should have, as much as I want to win it now. I'm two years stronger, two years more experienced, two years better, two years more of a man." He added, chillingly, "I would honestly rather lose my life in that ring than come out of it without the title."

There was little danger of that after he knocked Mattioli down in the first round and forced his man to quit after eight. Within another year Britain had three World Champions, all of them southpaws. Middle-weight Alan Minter and lightweight Jim Watt made up the trio, but of them all Hope looked the most complete. His manager, Terry Lawless, said, "The guys who spar against him always finish in a daze, not so much because he hurts them because Maurice never takes liberties, but because they can't work out where the punches are coming from."

Hope had three successful defences of his title. An American challenger, Mike Baker, in September 1979 showed guts, guile and a goodish punch, but Hope produced everything in the textbook of a fighting artist to stop him in seven rounds. After a long lay-off following an eye operation, he dismantled his old enemy Mattioli in eleven cold, clinical, punishing rounds. The third defence against a tough Argentinian, Carlos Herrera, was particularly important. Because the TV viewer was starting to take priority over the paying spectator this was staged in the early hours of the morning at Wembley on 26 November 1980 so that it could be screened live to the United States and shown on the same bill as Sugar Ray Leonard's attempt to regain the World Welterweight title from Roberto Duran.

The idea was to "sell" Maurice Hope to Americans as a future opponent for the winner because both Leonard and Duran were rumoured to be eyeing the light middleweight division hungrily. That is why Hope was for once allowed by his manager, the normally protective Lawless, to go into the ring less than one hundred per cent fit, weakened by a bout of 'flu. He had a rocky time against Herrera, lost a couple of early rounds, had the eighth taken away by American referee Arthur Mercante, and needed all his class and courage to win on points. It was the courage that encouraged his camp to feel they had landed the big one because that, incredibly, was what Duran had seemed to lack against Leonard. American fans were shocked and angered when Duran

*When an Italian opponent, Vincenzo Ungaro, tried to protect his head
Hope scored to the body. Mo won on a fifth-round knock-out.*

suddenly turned his back in the eighth round, flapping one glove in surrender and declaring "no more". He had been paid three million dollars and was later fined $3,000 for his performance and the feeling in England was that Hope would at least provide sterner opposition.

It was not to be. Leonard opted to go for the WBA version of the Light Middleweight title and although Mo Hope was paid big money to defend against the brilliant youngster Wilfred Benitez, there were no more huge paydays. Benitez, who made history when he became the youngest ever World Champion as a seventeen-year-old, fifteen-rounds points winner of the World Light Welterweight Championship against Antonio Cervantes in March 1976, was a 3–1 ringside favourite in Las Vegas in May 1981. That was not surprising. He had added the World Welterweight Championship by beating John Stracey's conqueror, Carlos Palomino.

Hope did not surrender his title lightly. He won the first four rounds and cut Benitez over one eye, but the arrogant young Puerto Rican slipped into a higher gear, solved Hope's southpaw style, knocked him down in the tenth, and then produced a truly awesome finishing punch in the twelfth round. That right cross was one of the most effective single punches ever seen. Hope dropped face first, then rolled on to his back and lay there for a full four minutes receiving attention. He was, in fact, never officially counted out. When he went down Lawless dived into the ring to make sure his fighter and his friend was all right. They wanted Hope to go out on a stretcher, but his pride prompted him to refuse and he insisted on walking into the ambulance for a hospital check-up that

Mattioli evades this right jab from Hope but a following left hook is on its way – and so is victory for Mo.

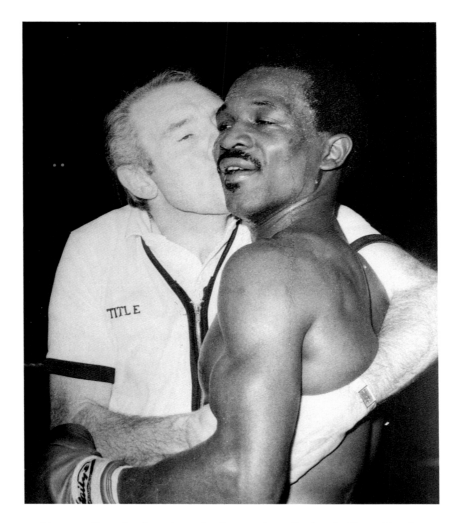

Manager Terry Lawless always had a genuine affection for Hope. Here he salutes a successful World Championship defence.

thankfully cleared him of brain damage.

In March 1982, with the legend "One Mo Time" emblazoned on the back of his gown, he tried for the European title and knew when the sheer strength of Italy's Luigi Minchinello cancelled out his own superior skill that it was all over. Lawless, who had managed more champions than any other Englishman, says, "They all needed different motivation in the corner – except Mo. He lived through so many disappointments and knew the game so thoroughly you just had to point him at the guy in the other corner and he did the rest. He was the easiest fighter I ever managed."

TED "KID" LEWIS
(1894 — 1970)

Ted "Kid" Lewis was paid perhaps the most notable compliment of the very many he accumulated during his long life, on the day it ended, 20 October 1970. A television announcer described him as "The best English fighter ever to visit the United States". Since few would argue about it, nor that Ted "Kid" Lewis was certainly the outstanding English fighter of this century, what made the accolade so remarkable and so lasting in the memory was that it was broadcast on an American TV programme in Atlanta, Georgia, where the rest of the sports news was dominated by Muhammad Ali's forthcoming comeback fight against Jerry Quarry.

That tells you something about the regard, respect, affection and awe the Americans still have for Ted "Kid" Lewis. It had been more than fifty years since he fought the second of two fights he had in Atlanta. It had been more than forty years since he last fought anywhere and America is not normally the most sentimental or even concerned of nations about British fighters. Also ask yourselves how many ex-American fighters who had died in their late seventies would be rated worth a mention by British television. Then you might agree it was a special tribute to a remarkable man.

The adjectives most frequently applied to the fighter and his style were dashing, bashing, crashing, smashing. If they evoke more recent images of Terry Downes that is because Ted "Kid" Lewis has always been seen as his role model. That is frankly flattering to Terry, even though he did win the World Middleweight title and go close to the light heavyweight crown in the sixties. Lewis fought 42 times for championships – almost as many as Downsie's career total of 44 fights. Lewis, in fact, had almost three hundred recorded fights from featherweight to heavyweight even though he seldom weighed more than 10 stone 12 lbs. He did, incidentally, meet and like Downes, but dismissed comparisons between them as scornfully as he felt they deserved. "He gets hit too easy. Me? I could take a punch but always felt it

Ted "Kid" Lewis sent a shudder of fear through many of the men who saw him coming at them. You can see why.

was smarter not to. I have always tried to hit the other guy first." He became famous for the sheer sustained ferocity of his attacks. And although the craggy face of the man as a long-retired veteran looked as though it had been splintered by a thousand punches he could not possibly have taken too much punishment or he would not have lasted so long nor been as lucid and lively in later life.

An examination of his career in the States reveals a breathtaking story of his non-stop whirlwind career. He had almost 100 fights in five years, travelling vast distances criss-crossing the continent. Twenty of those fights were against the only man capable of disputing his claim to be the best welterweight in the world, Philadelphia Jack Britton, the man from whom he first won the title in 1915. Between them they held

Even in repose, merely signing a contract to fight, Ted "Kid" Lewis still somehow manages to look menacing.

Lewis turns and walks away. He has seen it so many times before. This occasion was against Frankie Burns.

the title throughout his stay in the States, with Lewis winning three, losing five and drawing one. It was fifty years before another Briton won a welterweight title overseas – Ken Buchanan, the Scottish lightweight.

The rest of the Lewis v. Britton fights, all-action exchanges between two tigerishly aggressive men, were so-called "No Decision" affairs, peculiar to America at that time. Because professional boxing was officially outlawed in most States, the referee was not allowed to give a verdict – though on some occasions when Lewis was not fighting Britton the referee had to count to ten or stop the "exhibition". But because boxing was always enormously popular the "result" of the fights – and of all bets – depended on the verdict of sportswriters in the next day's newspapers. The gambler had to name the newspaper and the winner to get his money. Sportswriting has never been an easy profession. Sometimes in those days it was downright dangerous.

Lewis once fought Britton three times in twenty days in St Louis, New York and Dayton, Ohio, regaining the crown in the third fight. He was away from England for all the years of World War I but that did not seem to detract from his popularity when he returned in 1919 at the age of 25. Perhaps it was because no one in his right mind would query Lewis's physical courage. He was a man of intimidating mien all his life. And he was always revered rather than merely respected in his beloved East End of London, even during a spell in the 1930s when he took a job as bodyguard to the British Fascist leader Oswald Mosley, a strange occupation for a Jew, born Gershon Mendelhoff.

Johnny Sharpe, later to manage Terry Allen, the World Flyweight Champion, was a member of a very exclusive club – an opponent who beat Lewis. He outpointed Ted "Kid" Lewis in the first professional fight for both of them as fourteen-year-old flyweights. Ted always said his payment was sixpence but Sharpe denied it. "The reason I remember is that we were paid in coins in a dim little room. I thought they were half-crowns but they turned out to be pennies. I got fifteen and Ted got twelve, a shilling. He got double what he claimed so he's a liar." Then he added with a grin, "But for gawd's sake don't tell him I said so."

Lewis went on to become British Featherweight Champion at eighteen, by which time he had, according to the records, boxed over a hundred fights though he claimed there were even more. He sometimes boxed twice, even three times in the same week. He added the European championship and arrived in America via a successful tour of Australia in 1914. Within a year he was World Champion and by the time he returned to Britain was a seasoned warrior, more than merely intimidating. He was fearsome. He regained the British European and Empire Welterweight titles from a brilliant boxer, Johnny Basham, whose great skills simply could not survive such onslaughts. Few could.

He returned to America for one more successful challenge against Philadelphia Jack Britton, making the mistake of believing he could get out of a sick bed to fight another truly all-time great. But he was still King at home, not just for his fame but also for the fortune he was always prepared to squander cheerfully. At one time he estimated he used up a thousand pounds a week on "walking around" money.

His still almost outrageous self-belief that at under 11 stone he could take on the World Heavyweight Champion, Jack Dempsey, caused him to challenge for Georges Carpentier's World Light Heavyweight title. The reasoning was that if he could dispose of the great Frenchman more quickly than the four rounds it had taken Dempsey, he would become the obvious next opponent for the scowling, terrifying Manassa Mauler. The way Lewis was knocked out in the first round has become legend as the only time he overlooked the most basic law of a very hard game: "Defend yourself at all times." More than two inches shorter and two stone lighter he turned with his hands down to query an instruction from the referee and was caught relaxed and defenceless by a booming straight right that dropped him to his knees for the full count.

A return never materialised. Carpentier lost his title to Battling Siki, but Lewis still went on for another seven years fighting middleweights and upwards, winning six more titles and having his last fight in 1929 at the age of 35 against Johnny Basham. He won, but then that is always what Ted "Kid" Lewis was best at. Winning.

Johnny Basham was a brilliant boxer, but Lewis's whirling style overwhelmed him in twelve rounds.

ERNIE RODERICK
(1914 — 86)

Ernie Roderick, one of the best welterweights ever to come out of Merseyside's breeding ground of great champions, is that rarity – a man who earned, deserved and received a unique place in the affection and respect of the fans for a fight he could not and did not win. It was simply because at the end of a fifteen-round challenge for the World Welterweight title at Harringay on 25 May 1939 he was still on his feet.

To understand the extent of that achievement is to grasp how universally Henry Armstrong, the man who inevitably beat Roderick, is regarded as the most phenomenal fighter of all time. He was unique, the only man in boxing's history to hold three world titles simultaneously: featherweight (9 stone), lightweight (9 stone 9 lbs), welterweight (10 stone 7 lbs). He won them all inside fourteen months, from August 1937 to October 1938. In 41 winning fights during those two years only five men lasted the distance. He also boxed a controversial draw in a challenge for the World Middleweight title (11 stone 6 lbs) and if they had not at the time temporarily abandoned the in-between championships of super featherweight, light welterweight and light middleweight he would have won those also.

The man they called, with pardonable hyperbole, "Homicide Hank", had won his first title with a one-punch sixth-round knock-out of Petey Sarron, a great featherweight champion who had never previously been off his feet. Armstrong then jumped two divisions, deliberately quaffing gallons of beer to put on weight and then outpoint a noted hard man, Barney Ross, for the welterweight title – with Ross staying in his sick bed for three days after the fight. He moved back down to lightweight to dethrone Lou Ambers, despite having three rounds taken from him for low punching. His style was to start at a gallop and increase the pace. For his opponents it must have been like being caught in revolving doors which kept changing direction.

Roderick had become a highly respected British Welterweight Champion two months earlier at Anfield football ground, outboxing

Henry Armstrong watches intently as a doctor checks Roderick's heartbeat. The American knew how healthy his own was.

Roderick misses with a right swing and Armstrong's counter-punch to the body is already on its way.

Scotland's Jake Kilrain comprehensively with six rounds of left jabbing, then in the seventh banging across the right which saw the Scot counted out on his knees. A complaint by Kilrain that he could not hear the count for the crowd noise was nonsense – the referee was bawling it at him.

The new champion was an extremely capable, thoroughly experienced man of 25, in his prime, a crisp puncher with a long winning record built up over eight years, mainly in the North, and able to look after himself in most circumstances – but then Armstrong definitely rated in the class of an exceptional circumstance. It was his habit to shadow-box furiously for a full twenty minutes in his dressing room, working up a dripping sweat and speeding up the beat of an unusually large, slow-pumping heart. This was the source of his inexhaustible energy, the reason he was able to maintain such a bewildering pace, with punches of all kinds pouring non-stop from every angle.

Yet, astonishingly, it was Roderick who won the first round. It was a false dawning of hope. Although Roderick was taller and more than ten pounds heavier he was then caught up and swept around by the hurricane of punches that forced him to retreat to the ropes through succeeding rounds with only occasional one-punch counters. He did have a good eleventh round, but took so much out of himself in that rally, his corner ducked his head into the bucket at the bell. He may have shared the thirteenth in a final desperate fling but from then on sheer survival was the name of his exhausted game. Armstrong vaulted over the ropes and ran all the way back to the dressing room.

Roderick missed his chance of making a fortune – and, because he was always a top class performer, probably another world championship chance during the war. Air raids meant an enforced restriction on the size of crowds in the big indoor arenas. Open-air promotions were risky affairs. But, in between his stint in the services, he managed a couple of defences. He needed all his skill to survive the last three rounds against a big puncher, Norman Snow, at Northampton Rugby ground in July 1940, but had piled up so many points that the boos of disappointed locals were more an indication of partisanship than knowledge.

He did have a little bit of luck in a 1941 defence at the Albert Hall against Arthur Danahar. The Londoner looked much healthier as a welterweight than he had when he lost to Eric Boon in a pre-war championship fight at lightweight – the extra pounds were all muscle on a once skinny frame – and two top class boxers were evenly matched for ten rounds. Roderick's good fortune came early on when Danahar sportingly ignored a blatant low punch and waved the champion on, but the ring is no place to display gratitude. Danahar was knocked down by stiff rights twice in the thirteenth and did well to go the distance.

The Middleweight title had been vacant all through the war following the retirement of the great Jock McAvoy and Roderick eagerly grabbed the chance to fight a years younger and half-a-stone heavier Vince Hawkins for it, in May 1945. Hawkins was cut in the fifth, knocked down by the perfect one-two, left hook and right cross in the eighth. He won only two of the fifteen rounds at the Albert Hall, but a year later, a year stronger, better and more experienced, Hawkins at 23 took that title away from the 32-year-old Roderick.

He went wisely back to the welterweight division where, in Paris in February 1947, he dropped the European Welterweight title he had taken from Omar Kouidri, an Algerian, the previous year. The first challenger, Robert Villemain, was one of those fighters who has to be hurt to wake up and when he did he waded through everything Roderick threw. The Liverpudlian was forced to retire with terrible cuts after nine rounds.

Roderick still had too much polished ringcraft for two British title challengers, Gwyn Williams and Eric Boon, though he needed every ounce of it in a tremendous points win over Boon at Harringay in December 1947. Roderick was a mile in front after ten rounds but "Boy" Boon, armoured by his own courage to walk through Roderick's jabs and with bludgeoning force in both fists, gave him a torrid time. He cut the Champion's eye and had him down for a count of seven in the twelfth, caught and hurt the Liverpudlian in every succeeding round but could not put him away.

Roderick bitterly disputed the points defeat at 34 by the 26-year-old from Sheffield, Henry Hall, who finally took the title he had held for an impressive nine years, at Harringay in November 1948. It was close, but more significant is the fact that at his best he would certainly have destroyed a man who was never much more than mediocre. Points defeats in fights against men who were both to become holders of the welterweight championship he had come to think of as his property – Eddie Thomas and Cliff Curvis – prompted inevitable retirement at the age of 36 in 1950 when he became the first Lonsdale belt holder to qualify for the £1 a week pension it then carried with it. He should never have needed it. If there had not been a Henry Armstrong around he might even have retired richer as a former champion of the world.

Henry Hall slips inside this left jab from Roderick, who always insisted he
landed enough of them to have kept his title.

PETER WATERMAN
(1934 — 86)

Peter Waterman, Welterweight Champion of Britain and Europe was jogging gently through a training run across the common near his Clapham home one spring evening when he was stopped, jostled and threatened by two young toughs of a familiar type. They were flashy, menacing, fancied themselves a little and were looking for trouble. Now Peter could be rather spiteful in the ring, a waspish puncher and with a deserved reputation for bravery, so when he told the story after a training session in the gymnasium a couple of days later, an over-eager questioner jumped in to ask how severely he had spanked nuisances who can be the bane of a professional fighter's life – nonentities hoping to achieve a little notoriety.

Peter, an intelligent, educated, literate man, said scornfully, "Oh do leave off. No way would I have a punch-up, hurt my hands. I get paid for fighting with gloves on and a referee. Nah, I *talked* them out of it." There are echoes in that dialogue of the lines his younger brother, actor Dennis Waterman, speaks in his role as "Minder" to George Cole's Arthur Daley. And the way Dennis's Terry McCann throws those two nice little consecutive left hooks, one underneath to the body, the second whipped in to the head, in so many fight scenes, indicates that he had a close-to-home role model. It was always a favourite attacking ploy of the real-life fighter.

Peter Waterman had been a distinguished amateur, turning professional at eighteen in 1952 after winning an ABA title - and very swiftly adapting a totally orthodox style to the more crowd-pleasing approach that punching for pay demands of its practitioners. He very quickly built up a string of thirty consecutive wins and created with it a reputation for ruthlessness. Few have ever been quicker to get in again with a left hook when a referee broke up a clinch. Opponents would often find themselves on the floor trying to get ready to box on. Thirty of his 41 fights ended inside the distance and he lost only three.

Approaching his 21st birthday he showed he was ready for a title fight, when he tackled a tough Portuguese, Raphael da Silva, who had been in with seven European champions to stay the course each time. That left hook knocked da Silva out in the second round when he had already been down for nine. Waterman was promised a British title fight with champion Wally Thom at Harringay on 7 February 1956 and when the southpaw Thom broke his punching fist, the left, against the head of a Frenchman, the youngster was bitterly disappointed until promoter Jack Solomons promised to bring in "a world class American" instead to top the bill.

Fight-wise customers, who had heard all that before, yawned but woke up and started rushing for tickets when the opponent was announced as Kid Gavilan, an all-time great. Born in Cuba, christened Gerardo Gonzalez and nicknamed "The Hawk", this superb boxer was 30 years old but not nearly over the hill when he came to London. He had been World Champion not much more than a year and had more than a hundred victories. He had fought all the top men in the world and beaten most of them. He would have been a handful for any of the very best from the welterweight division of any era at their best. Waterman was an infant by comparison.

A swinging left from Gavilan is on its way to Waterman's ribs in the fight that went controversially to Peter.

Emilio Marconi of Italy avoided this right cross from Waterman, but still lost his European title.

Gavilan's speciality was the so-called "bolo" punch, a sort of whirling right uppercut which he said he had developed cutting sugar cane for a living in his native land. And the fans loved it. Waterman became the victim of probably the worst decision ever seen in a British ring when the referee, the veteran Ben Green, lifted Peter's arm in victory to astound and anger the spectators at the end of ten rounds. Waterman, not Gavilan, was the victim because a brave, potentially brilliant prospect never got any credit yet, in fact, did deserve some. He made a great start to the fight and was in front by the third. No one else at Harringay that night apart from Ben Green thought Waterman won another round.

There were the wise guys, of course, who said that Gavilan fought only in flurries, husbanding his energies and cutting loose for only about a minute in every round. But what he did to Waterman during those minutes provided a painful lesson about every punch in the book including one, that "bolo", which did not exist in any other fighter's repertoire. Gavilan's manager, an excitable Spaniard called Yamil Chade, tried to attack the white-haired, tubby veteran referee and had to be restrained again in the dressing room when he was demanding to be given that official's address. Green's decision, incidentally, forced the Board to introduce a new rule imposing an age limit of 65 on referees, which caused his immediate retirement – at 68.

The calmest man in the place was Gavilan who said, "I have had many bad decisions. Every fighter gets those sometimes, though this is the worst I have known. I will, of course, fight your Waterman again and certainly I would come back to London to fight him because the way the crowd reacted means they would not dare to do such a thing again. Besides, I think the peoples will wish to see it."

He was, of course, right. "The peoples" were available in such numbers that Solomons booked the giant Earls Court Arena for the return two months later when Waterman actually did rather better. He lost on points inevitably but, second time around, was good enough to share the points up to the end of the seventh – then Gavilan clicked into a higher gear and honour was satisfied.

Waterman was still only 21, still full of potential, and one of the best judges of boxing in Britain recognised it. Wally Thom became a star class referee eventually, one of the small select band considered good enough to handle championship fights, and it was that same generous-hearted Liverpudlian who did a great deal to restore Peter Waterman's self-esteem. Waterman, cold-eyed and confident, had taken all Thom's best shots in a championship challenge and then took his title also by busting up and cutting Thom so badly that he had to retire in the fifth round. The 30-year-old Thom then walked over to him in the corner at Harringay in May 1956 and said, "Listen to me, son. I really believe you have it in you to become one of the great champions."

No one then realised there was not much ring-time remaining. Waterman beat two more top men that year, a former European champion, Idrissa Dione, on points and forced the former Lightweight Champion, Frank Johnson of Manchester, to retire in ten rounds. He wrestled the European Champion, Emilio Marconi, to a draw the following year, then took that title also in a return, stopping the Italian with cuts after a bruising fight in January 1958. But his style was changing significantly, and when the lighter but stronger and fitter Dave Charnley stopped him in five rounds – only the third defeat of his career – he retired. Micky Duff observed shrewdly at the time, "When a fighter keeps going forward but leaves his arms behind that's the signal to quit." What nobody else knew was that Peter Waterman was already afflicted by a nervous system ailment that would contribute to his tragically early death. The saddened world of boxing made sure there was one more full house for him at his memorial service.

JOHN H. STRACEY
(1950 —   )

John H. Stracey was the cockney kid who was almost as proud of his homeland as he was of becoming World Welterweight Champion. He did not just stand to attention when they played the National Anthem in the hot and hostile atmosphere of Mexico City's Plaza de Toros, the 55,000-seater biggest bullring in the world on 6 December 1975. He filled his lungs, threw back his head and bellowed the words in a defiant gesture directed at the menacing man in the opposite corner.

José "Mantequilla" Napoles is still rated an all-time great, with probably only Sugar Ray Robinson his superior in the welterweight division he had ruled for six years. There were those who doubted the wisdom of Stracey's manager, Terry Lawless, normally notoriously protective of his fighters, in signing for the fight. But there was a story behind that story. "Mantequilla" Napoles – the nickname is Spanish for butter, smooth and slippery – was 35 years old, had been fighting and winning, usually by sudden concussive knock-outs, since he was eighteen in his native Cuba. The previous year he had taken the only real beating of his distinguished career when he was cut to pieces by another great world champion from a higher division, Carlos Monzon, five inches taller and a stone heavier. In an earlier 1975 defence Napoles had one eye closed and both cut. It was, in fact, a new rule that rescued his title because Napoles was well ahead on points when the fight was stopped in the twelfth for "accidental butting" by opponent Armando Muniz, who went the distance in a return and was agitating for a third chance.

Lawless took the fight only because he thought someone else might get to and beat Napoles first and, of course, because he felt that Napoles might not have too much left. That idea went right out of the window in the opening round when Napoles hit Stracey on the chin with a left hook as good as any he ever triggered. Stracey himself said afterwards, "I didn't see it or feel it. I just heard the referee count three." But he was good enough to be back in it by the end of the round. The fight became rough, tough and nasty. Napoles stuck his thumb in Stracey's eye and butted him. Stracey butted right back and, when Napoles slipped in the third, hit the Mexican-Cuban twice while he was on the floor. Ruthlessness is a rare asset in an Englishman.

Clearly this one was never going the distance with Mantequilla's right eye cut and closing from the third round and a great champion putting it all together in clusters to get rid of the young champion he had dismissed with such extravagant contempt before the fight: "Stracey is a naughty baby who has has climbed out of his cot. I will smack his bottom and put him back." He suspected how wrong he was during the fourth when Stracey actually turned to his corner and laughed out loud. Napoles really knew it in the sixth when he cracked a perfect right to the chin and Stracey did not even blink. He walked through it to mount a final assault which hammered Napoles into the ropes. The total of hooks, jabs and crosses pounded by Stracey to his unprotected head and checked later on a TV replay amounted to the fearsome total of 25 and the referee had to stop the fight. Several minutes later Napoles was half-carried, half-dragged to his dressing room into retirement.

John H. Stracey had always believed that a world title was not just a dream but his destiny, though it had been a long road. It had started coincidentally in that same Mexico City, where he had been a member of Britain's Olympic team. At just turned eighteen, he was the baby of a boxing squad, which included another future champion, Chris Finnegan.

He won an ABA title at light welterweight at eighteen in 1969 and turned professional with Terry Lawless just after his nineteenth birthday. By the time he was 22 he was British Welterweight Champion, knocking out Bobby Arthur with a perfect one-punch finish, a right cross in the fourth round at the Albert Hall in 1973. He and many boxing enthusiasts thought that he had knocked out Arthur to win the title eight months earlier, in seven rounds with a perfect body blow. The referee had ruled it low, however, and disqualified him, but it did not seem to matter much. He improved steadily, showing only one fault – a fighting heart that sometimes overruled a cool boxing brain and lured him into unnecessary wars.

When a European welterweight title fight was mooted against a good champion, Roger Menetrey of France, who had won his crown from another Lawless fighter, Ralph Charles, in 1971 and defended it a menacing five times, the manager wanted to wait. Stracey travelled to see Menetrey in action and said to Lawless, "You get it on and I'll get it over." In May 1974 he travelled to the Roland Garros Stadium in Paris and proved that his youthful confidence was justified. He had seen that Menetrey was a roundhouse swinger and punched the straightest

Stracey, determined not to risk his world ranking was ruthless all through the six rounds it took to stop a Swiss, Max Hebeisen.

distance between two points, his fists and the Frenchman's head, so often and so effectively that the referee stopped it in the eighth round.

Promoters were already talking about Napoles when Stracey went down with appendicitis and his first defence of the European title was almost a year after he won it and six months after his most recent fight. He knew he had to clear that hurdle against a Swiss, Max Hebeisen. It proved to be a formality in April 1975 against a man who could move backwards almost as fast as Stracey moved forwards – and the operative word is almost. Stracey caught up with a character who operated behind the shell of a high close-fisted guard in the sixth. He produced a comparatively rare punch, a left uppercut that scrambled Hebeisen's senses and battered him to defeat.

Stracey said, "I hadn't dared to think about Napoles until I got over this hurdle. Now I'll think about nothing else" – but even he did not know how close Lawless came to calling off that world title fight. The manager was incensed when the Mexicans broke their promise of a neutral referee, refused Lawless's demand for another £5,000 on the £20,000 purse, rejected another Lawless offer to accept £5,000 less if they would climb down and when he threatened to pull out said they had a stand-by challenger ready. In the end, Stracey's fists made a referee almost unnecessary and he was cock of the walk, king of the heap. Although he had trouble in the early rounds of his first defence against the brilliant if flashy American Hedgemon Lewis, a man part-owned by film star Ryan O'Neal, Stracey eventually totally overwhelmed him with superior punching and stopped him in style in the tenth round in March 1976.

He made an equally brilliant start to his next defence, cracking home a terrific left hook to the head of Mexican-American Carlos Palomino at Wembley three months later. It would have knocked out most, but, though he wobbled, Palomino came back to outpunch Stracey and stop him with wicked body shots in the twelfth round. It was an off-night for Stracey who had been lapping up the popularity his talent and personality warranted.

He still craved the big time and there was still big money in a fight the fans saw as a repeat of Boon v. Danahar against the up and coming brawler from Chatteris, Dave "Boy" Green. The phone in Lawless's gym never stopped ringing from fans wanting handfuls of tickets without even asking the prices. For nine rounds it was worth it, that night at Wembley in March 1977. Stracey, half-blinded by cuts in the fifth, came back in the eighth and ninth so fiercely he looked like swinging it, but it was a gambler's last throw. He was hurt by rib-busters in the tenth and rescued by the referee. The time that comes to them all had arrived for him. Time to go.

Stracey had all the confidence of a newly crowned champion when he stopped Hedgemon Lewis in ten one-sided rounds.

LLOYD HONEYGHAN
(1 9 6 0 —   )

Only one cocky, flashy man in the boxing world genuinely believed that Lloyd Honeyghan would beat Donald "The Cobra" Curry from Fort Worth, Texas, the undisputed Welterweight Champion of the world, in Atlantic City on 27 September 1986. Every expert was agreed that the American was already one of the sport's immortals, not merely undefeated but unbeatable.

The solitary, scornful heretic was, no prizes for guessing, the same Lloyd Honeyghan, who had been growing steadily more restless, bitter and angry at the critics, one of whom compared him with a Fourth Division team going for the World Cup; at the open contempt of Curry who insisted that Honeyghan's record "against old men and youngsters with limited skills" did not entitle him to share the same ring; and at the bookmakers who made him a 6–1 underdog. They studied only Curry's unbeaten record, which then included seven successful world title defences in less than thirty rounds. Honeyghan studied the films and the facts of those victories. "No one has ever made him fight on the retreat," he said. "I'll do it." He did too - almost from the start and by the fifth round the Cobra was slithering backwards being caught and hurt constantly by swift long right-hand punches. In the sixth round one of them cut his eye and Honeyghan chased, harried and hurt him, outpunching him at least two to one.

It is significant that Curry made no objections when it was stopped at the end of that round. Nor, having insisted he was comfortable at the weight, was he interested in a return. He immediately moved into the Light Middleweights where he has never seemed as majestic and invincible again. Yet it is difficult to condemn anyone, the critics, Curry or the bookies, for failing to invest Honeyghan with those same qualities of majesty and invincibility despite his own unbeaten record. There had been no sudden meteoric rise in the rankings for the youngster who turned professional at twenty in 1980 after an unremarkable amateur career. You had to look way down in the small print of the British rankings to find him in fourteenth place at the start of 1983. He was just another up-and-coming eight-round fighter, who became suddenly lucky. He twice stepped in as a late substitute for British Welterweight title eliminators and the second of these against the equally obscure Cliff Gilpin of Telford was suddenly elevated to a full championship fight, at the Albert Hall, in April of that year when champion Kirkland Laing relinquished the title.

Honeyghan won the battle of the comparative nobodies, but Gilpin will always be able to tell future grandchildren, truthfully, that he had a World Champion in real trouble. Honeyghan was battered throughout the first round, knocked down in the second and wobbling when he went to his corner. It was only his sixteenth pro fight and to become a champion and remain undefeated he had to fight like one for another ten rounds. He won a return match far more convincingly eight months later, but hand injuries which have always plagued him kept him inactive through most of 1984.

He started the New Year brilliantly, going to Italy to knock out the reigning European Champion, Gianfranco Rosi, in the third round with one cracking right hand to the chin which sent the Italian unconscious through the ropes. He ended the year by outclassing Sylvester Mittee in eight rounds, regaining the British title he had relinquished and adding the Commonwealth title. That was under new management – after an acrimonious split from the tightly disciplined, highly organised and very successful Terry Lawless stable. There were stories of explosive squabbles including, it is claimed, one, when big Frank Bruno had to separate Honeyghan and Lawless's tough trainer at the time, Jimmy Tibbs.

Lawless, incidentally, never showed any regrets, resentments or recriminations after agreeing to – or rather insisting upon – the handing over of Honeyghan's contract to Micky Duff, a partnership which had survived some notable public clashes of egos, opinions and conflicts. Micky Duff, never short of a colourful quote, says, "There is no clause in the contract which states that Lloyd Honeyghan and I have to like each other, never mind one that says we should be friends". It is even arguable whether, with the notoriously cautious Lawless as his manager, Honeyghan would have been encouraged to fight a champion as great as Curry was reckoned to be – though by then another significant figure had joined the camp. Bobby Neill, probably the best teacher of boxing in the country, took over as Honeyghan's trainer, with an immediate improvement in both footwork and punching power.

Bobby's theory is that feet are as important as fists – "Because your feet take you where you can hurt and take you away from where you can

Micky Duff, Honeyghan's manager, says, "There is nothing in the contract that says we have to like each other." Lloyd agrees.

get hit. The power behind punches comes from the feet upwards, more than from the shoulders onwards." Honeyghan had always been a quick hitter, but not always an effective one. "He had to plant his feet to get the necessary leverage," says Neill. Bobby is bitter about the way he was subsequently discarded. He feels Honeyghan soaked up all the knowledge he had to offer and then had no further use for him – or made him feel so much a menial that he could take no more. But then Honeyghan never has tried very hard to present a "Mr Nice Guy" image.

Controversy has been an almost constant companion in his championship career. In his first defence of the International Boxing Federation title in February 1987 at Wembley against Johnny Bumphus, a six-footer with a reputation for pure skill, Bumphus never had a chance to display his boxing talents. Honeyghan climbed all over him in the first round, had him down for six and shaken. "Honey" was so keen to finish it that he rushed across at the start of the second and knocked Bumphus down as he was rising from his stool, prompting appeals for disqualification. It was stopped shortly after, with Bumphus drooping over the ropes – and out of the fight game.

The authentic, all-action, aggressive Honeyghan was just starting to emerge as this 1985 victory over Robert Smith illustrated.

Only two months later, Honeyghan, keeping his promise to be an active champion, had a harder job outpointing another American, Maurice Blocker, but the verdict was unanimous, with blazing aggression the clinching factor. In Marbella in August there was another sensation, an official world record. Honeyghan's destruction in forty seconds, including two counts, of a third American, Gene Hatcher, was the fastest ever in any world championship fight. Hatcher was down from the first punch and knocked out by the blizzard of blows that then fell on him.

Honeyghan had already caused headlines when he threatened to quit 48 hours before the Blocker fight in an argument about money. He did the same after his first ever defeat in October 1987 against a Mexican Jorge Vaca, who was not remotely in the same class. It ended in controversy with Vaca the victim in the eighth round of "accidental butting", which, under a new and strange rule, meant that Honeyghan had one point deducted and, because he was trailing on the score-cards of two judges, was adjudged the split-decision loser on points. Once again Micky Duff was the subject of a tirade by Honeyghan, who blamed the manager for persuading him to carry on with the fight when he alleged he was "physically and mentally not ready". Both excuses are believable because Honeyghan has a medical history of hand injuries and, as for his so-called "personal problems", at the last count he had fathered five children for three different mothers, which most would find a distinctly disturbing set of circumstances.

During the course of all this, Honeyghan had been stripped of the WBA version of the title for refusing to fight in South Africa against one Harold Volbrecht. The Los Angeles Olympic Champion, Mark Breland, went instead to take that crown and a huge money match against him was temporarily shelved by Vaca. Honeyghan, not surprisingly, had little trouble in knocking out Vaca in three rounds in a return fight in March 1988 but, by then, Breland had dropped his title to Marlon Starling. Still, there was going to be big money for Honeyghan against him instead, in what was being built up nicely as a grudge fight after Starling called Honeyghan "an over-rated street-fighting punk". Honeyghan took considerable exception to this remark.

The astonishing events in Atlantic City, New Jersey, in July 1988 caused that fight to be shelved also. Starling was knocked out so long after the bell rang to end the sixth round against a Colombian Tomas Molinares that an appeal against the referee, who started and finished a count to ten, was immediately and justifiably launched. On the same bill – for the purely commercial reason of whipping up interest in a future fight against Starling – Honeyghan was named as the winner by a technical knock-out of a Korean, Yunk Kil Chung, in 42 seconds of the fifth round. What really happened was that the Korean was fouled and felled by a left hook so low that it travelled up between his thighs before crunching home. He insisted he was still too sick to continue after five minutes' rest and recuperation and another row raged.

Honeyghan will, undoubtedly, be recognised as the most controversial World Champion England has ever produced. But when the definitive history is written he should also be rightfully recognised as one of the very best.

Maurice "Thin Man" Blocker was a brave and skilful opponent, but Honeyghan's naked aggression was the clinching winning factor.

TERRY MARSH
(1 9 5 8 —)

No fighter ever had a career cut short more cruelly and at greater financial cost than Terry Marsh. By September 1987, he had won and defended the International Boxing Federation World Welterweight title. He had taken over the keys to a bank vault with licence to plunder when, at 29, the door was slammed shut and bolted by doctors who discovered he suffered, if only mildly and intermittently, from a form of epilepsy. When he also had to abandon a career in the Fire Service that meant as much to him, the world of anyone less resilient might have collapsed.

But Marsh always had an engaging ambivalence about fighting for a living anyway. He was already 23 when he turned professional and scoffed at what he called "dreams of glory rubbish". His intentions at that time were a lot like the style which served him more than adequately as an amateur – get in first, pick up what he could with a fast left hand and get out before he got hurt. He was bright academically, with eight 'O' Levels, and studying at external college for a cluster of 'A's. He had been junior chess champion of London at the age of eleven – and applied the same sort of intellect to his sport. To him boxing was chess with bruises and the fewer of those he collected, the better. "The theory is the same," he insisted. "You probe for weaknesses and nullify strengths."

Amateur honours came regularly – he was National Schools Champion, Boys Club Champion, Junior ABA Champion twice, ABA Senior Champion three times and runner-up once while he was doing a four-year stint in the Royal Marines. Disillusion set in when that important haul of titles failed to win him selection for the 1980 Olympic Games in Moscow.

There were many who doubted whether an apparently fragile frame and that quick orthodox style would survive against the tougher bangers in the professional game. Such men tend to treat left jabs like hamburgers, eating them up and ploughing on to punish without pausing. One distinguished Sunday paper columnist who suggested something like that might happen to Marsh was given a public rough ride when, at a Boxing Writers' Club dinner, guest speaker Terry singled him out. It was as unwise to cross verbal swords with Marsh as it was to venture into a ring against him. He once debated at the Cambridge Union against some distinguished professors from the British Medical Association and won so convincingly that the delighted students heavily supported his view against a motion "This House would Ban Boxing". If the contest had been in a ring the referee would have stopped it. Marsh won by 135 votes to 50.

Marsh was certainly the quickest-witted, best provider of one-liners in British boxing, summing up his own initial unbeaten run of fifteen fights at the start of his career with a dry, "I went fifteen contests on the trot undetected". The sixteenth made the sport take rather more notice when, against the odds, he convincingly outpointed the tougher and vastly more experienced Clinton McKenzie to win the British Light Welterweight title in September 1984. McKenzie, with only brief interruptions, had been Champion for more than five years in that division, but Marsh took all his damaging body punches without wilting.

The vital proof that he could provide a Jekyll and Hyde transformation in style came during his challenge for the European title just over a year later against Italy's Alessandro Scapecchi. Although Marsh broke a bone in his trusty left jabbing hand, he kept going smoothly, until a butt gashed him so badly that the referee called the ringside doctor to examine the wound before allowing the fight to go into the sixth round. "I knew he was getting ready to stop it," said Marsh – so orthodox boxing had to go out of the window. Marsh became a two-fisted one-man assault force battering Scapecchi to his knees for a count and, when the Italian rose, wobbling and dazed, resuming so enthusiastically that it was stopped. He had found another way to fight. The fans, in their turn, had found a way to warm to the newly crowned European Champion.

He successfully defended the title against an African-born Frenchman, Tusikoleta Nkalankete, at Alexandra Palace, in January 1986 when, in fact, mixing styles turned out to be a mistake and Marsh had a rough ride to his points victory. He won all twelve rounds next time out against another Italian, Francesco Prezisio, in the Isle of Man three months later. But boxing as far as he was concerned provided no more than the jam on his bread-and-butter job. Fire-fighting, he insisted, was his real career. Marsh's greatest delight from boxing was his unbeaten record. "I suppose it is a bit like your virginity. Things can't ever be the same once you've lost it." Most of the experts thought that would

*Terry Marsh, always a great kidder, turned himself into a southpaw for
this gymnasium picture, but fought correctly when it counted.*

happen when, for the first time, he had a chance to make a fireman's annual wages look small against a purse for one night's work. It was a challenge for the International Boxing Federation version of the World Light Welterweight title held by a strong muscular man from the tough streets of Detroit, Michigan, USA.

Joe Louis Manley was named, like his father before him, after a great world champion though personally he idolised another later less great Heavyweight Champion on whom he modelled his style, Joe Frazier. Marsh was well aware of that fact when they met in the ring set up in a circus tent at Basildon, Essex, on 4 March 1987, a date that coincided with his fifth wedding anniversary to wife Jackie and the third birthday of their daughter Kelly.

It was "the other Terry Marsh", all snarling aggression, who exploded into fighting fury again that night – with a tinge of psychological warfare thrown in. Manley had revealed that, as he fought, the words "Frazier, Frazier, Frazier" pumped from his mind, through his nerve ends, into the rhythm of his punches, so, in the seventh round of a non-stop pounding, Marsh pulled him into a clinch and whispered, "Joe Frazier can't help you now." He had the wilting Manley down at the end of the ninth and within twenty seconds of the tenth left-hooked him to the floor again. He just beat the count, but one look into suddenly empty eyes and referee Randy Neumann stopped it.

There was a similar touch of psychology during Terry's defence against Akio Kamede of Japan in July, four months later at the Albert Hall. At one stage Marsh, with cuts around both eyes, but full of confidence, raised his arms, allowed his opponent three, free, clear, full-strength shots at the body and just grinned ferociously. Kamede was stopped at the end of the sixth round and Terry, this time with a genuine grin, said, "He almost broke my ribs, but I knew damn well I had broken his heart."

A fortune awaited – £250,000 for his next defence – but Marsh had known for two years about his medical condition, quite wrongly concealing it and the decision to quit could not be delayed, though he lost a once-valued friendship with his promoter-manager Frank Warren, first for keeping the secret and then for selling it to a newspaper. The money he missed in his boxing career may, however, one day seem like small change to him as he embarks on a new one – as commentator, after-dinner speaker, actor, businessman, promoter, entrepreneur. He has a quality already mentioned – resilience.

MATT WELLS
(1886 — 1953)

Only one thing could ever anger Matt Wells, the former British Lightweight Champion and briefly Welterweight Champion of the world. That was any modern champion not sharing the dedication for boxing he himself always had. He served the sport he loved and respected to the end of his days. Literally hundreds of young boxers came under his educated old eyes, passed through his hands and were grateful for the wisdom he was always willing to share. Among them, for instance, in the late 1940s was one Henry Cooper, then in his early teens. Matt taught him and brother George the basics of boxing for four years and Henry proved a distinguished ex-pupil.

Talking of Cooper always leads somehow to Harry Gibbs. That great referee, robbed of a professional career during wartime years by being penned behind barbed wire in a German POW camp – though he did have seven, and won six, paid fights – tells his own rueful story about Matt Wells. "I always reckon it was old Matt who may have prevented me winning the ABA Light Heavyweight title just after the war. I got beat in a divisional final by a feller from Lynn Athletic where Matt was a trainer who really knew the game. He had spotted that I could jab a bit and sent his boy out to get stuck in right away. It worked, I got stopped. The other boy got to the ABA final."

It was at that same Lynn Athletic club, in Walworth, South London, around the turn of the century that Matt Wells started his career. His story differs, in fact, from that of so many others of that era because he stayed in the amateur ranks to win four successive national titles from 1904 to 1907. The main reason he turned professional in the first place at the comparatively late age of 23 was the difficulty of finding opponents who could provide any sort of test.

Nothing much changed when he started winning cash rather than cutlery, so off he went to the States for a year to toughen and polish his talent, preparation for the night when he achieved a place among the immortals of the game, when he outpointed Freddie Welsh over twenty

Gymnasium conditions were very basic back in 1919, but Matt Wells still got himself fit enough at 33 to go twenty rounds.

rounds at the National Sporting Club. Welsh, born Frederick Thomas, came from Pontypridd and was unquestionably one of the very best fighters to leave the principality - right up there with Jimmy Wilde and Peerless Jim Driscoll - though he did, in all truth, leave his native Wales further behind him than either. The vast majority of Welsh's 168 fights over seventeen years from 1905 until 1922 were in America. He lost only four, and that is an unusual feat.

While Matt was in the States learning his trade, Freddie had returned to mop up all available British opposition - and made himself vastly unpopular at times. In the fight before he met Wells he had so enraged Jim Driscoll with his holding, clinching and wrestling - ruining what should have been a glorious spectacle - that Driscoll lost his head. Infuriated at a failure to get that famous left jab going, he butted Welsh so blatantly that it brought him disqualification for the first and only time in his career.

Welsh, reckoned to be a cold, aloof character, was not a popular fighter with the fans. But he was a definite betting favourite with the realists, the ringside gamblers who reckoned he was sufficiently superior to start at 4-1 on. Wells, a comparative novice, was felt to have only two outside chances on that February night in 1911. Welsh might get disqualified, though it seemed unlikely, and Matt's other chance of a one-punch knock-out seemed even more remote. Welsh had already won more than seventy fights and had never even been floored. The prospect of a points victory for the underdog was not even considered. Welsh even wore an amused smile for the first couple of rounds – though that soon disappeared. At long range he liked to circle his man, dictating the pace, the flow, the direction of a fight with his jabs – yet, in the event, that is precisely what Wells did to him. At close quarters Welsh always wanted to get inside an opponent's arms, tuck his chin on the other guy's shoulder, rip in hooks to the body and uppercuts to the head. Wells took that play away from him also and the crowd actually laughed at the way the Welshman's own game was being outrageously stolen.

Some of Matt's genuine enthusiasm for "The Hardest Game" shines through another 1919 training picture.

By the fifteenth, Freddie needed a knock-out and knew it. He was having to do all the chasing. The closest he got was when he, they say accidentally, brought his knee up during a clinch into Matt's groin in the seventeenth. The Englishman's protests were ignored and he looked shaky throughout the eighteenth, but he fought back to take the nineteenth and the ringside betting odds told their own incredible story. If you wanted to back Freddie Welsh coming into the twentieth and last you could name your own odds. Matt Wells was the new British Lightweight Champion.

The return, delayed by further transatlantic trips by both, in November 1912, was much closer, with Freddie's defence tighter and his in-fighting improved. His points win was disputed by Matt because Freddie had a tendency to slap, but Wells did not get another chance. Welsh returned immediately to the States and Wells, growing into a welterweight, went to Australia in search instead of the world title in that division. It was in chaos at the time, mainly because, as an editorial in *Boxing* pointed out sardonically: "All that any American boxer needs to do is go around shouting he is the champion." In the event, a tough Dane, Waldemar Holberg, beat one such American claimant, Ray Bronson, in Melbourne and was recognised as Champion. Holberg lost it three weeks later on a disqualification against an Irishman, Tom McCormick, in the same city. Wells, who had already knocked out Bronson in seven rounds, convincingly outpointed McCormick over twenty rounds and achieved his own dream in Sydney in March 1914.

Wells took the World Welterweight title to America where he lost it to Mike Glover on points over fifteen rounds in Boston in 1915 and stayed on for a series of mainly "No Decision" contests until his return to England in 1919 to take on the best of British welterweights. By then he was 33 - and they were too much for him. The brilliant Johnny Basham outpointed him over twenty rounds. The great Ted "Kid" Lewis battered him inside twelve rounds - on Boxing Day, incidentally.

Matt fought on until his 36th year in 1922 but, even then, did not hang up his gloves. For many years he pulled them on regularly to teach what for him was truly a Noble Art, to Guy's Hospital students, to Dulwich College schoolboys - in the days before it was decided that boxing was not character building for youngsters - to police cadets in the Metropolitan Police - where an ability to look after himself can come in handy for a young copper - and at his beloved Lynn Athletic club.

JACK "KID" BERG
(1 9 0 9 —)

Meeting Jack "Kid" Berg in the ring could be a bewildering, strenuous and very painful ordeal as one man with first-hand experience of the character could testify. Berg's style was vividly captured in his nickname – "The Whitechapel Whirlwind" – and Mushy Callahan, an extrovert American pugilist from whom Berg had won the World Junior Welterweight title in London in 1930, told a delightful, if possibly apocryphal, story. Required to provide on an official form two reasons why he felt he should be excused service on a jury, which could cost him time and money, Mushy said he wrote simply "Jackie Kid Berg. Twice."

For him that said it all. Whenever they rang a bell Berg always exploded into action and became a blur of blows on two legs, swarming all over anyone they put in front of him. Callahan had already faced that fury once in his native New York and lost on points in a non-title fight. Agreeing to come to London with his championship at stake was, if not lunacy, certainly not a sign of the cool judgement any defendant would want from a member of the jury. Berg literally finished him in ten rounds which ended with Callahan exhausted on his stool and deciding to quit boxing. He never fought again. At the time the British Boxing Board of Control were possibly correct to withhold world championship recognition from Berg. They treated an artificially created division at 10 stone with justified suspicion, even disdain. But they were wrong to persist in that attitude when it was an Englishman – that same Jack "Kid" Berg – who brought status, respectability, dignity, even honour, to it with his savagery, bravery and skill.

Berg became only the third holder of a crown that initially was not much more than a publicity stunt. The first Champion, one Myron Pinkey Mitchell, was actually elected to the position in 1922 by a poll of readers of a publication called *The Boxing Blade* – edited, incidentally, by his own manager. No one took much notice when Callahan won the title from Pinkey Mitchell in 1926.

It was Berg who made people take notice by defending the championship successfully an astonishing nine times in America in 1930 and 1931. Every fight was an all-action war with Berg frequently taking below the belt blows under the rule which insisted that fights could not be won on a disqualification. Not that he ever complained – he was not always too worried about where his own punches landed. The toughness of his background and upbringing provides the reason why. He was born Judah Bergman in Whitechapel in 1909, to the sort of poverty which makes fighting for a living come naturally. He was boxing professionally at the age of fourteen and by the time he was eighteen was competing regularly against British and European champions, so successfully that he decided to try his luck in America. He had already had almost sixty fights. Often, as was quite common in those days, there was only a week, sometimes even less, between them. The attitude of a youngster as carefree and extrovert as The Kid was, "It beats training". That chirpy cockney confidence was his shield against what to most at his age must have been strange and daunting.

He became "perhaps the finest fighter ever sent across the Atlantic". That is a direct quote from *Boxing News* Editor Harry Mullan's *Illustrated History of Boxing*, one of the most comprehensive and meticulously researched volumes written on the sport. Equally certainly the claims of only one other Englishman, also Jewish, the great Ted "Kid" Lewis, could be put forward in contention. Berg fought and beat a succession of genuine world-class men in 1930, the year of his 21st birthday. Among them were the legendary Cuban "Kid" Chocolate who had won sixty fights in a row until he came up against The Kid and Tony Canzoneri, who was to capture the World Lightweight title later that same year.

It was Canzoneri, in fact, who claimed Berg's title on a night in April 1931 when for once the Englishman's style caused his own downfall. Coming forward at speed as usual his impetus doubled the impact and effect of a cracking right to the jaw that KO'd him in three. Five months later, which saw Berg win six more tough fights, he had another crack at Canzoneri. Berg was knocked down twice in the first round, but got up to be ahead by the eighth when a low punch almost crippled him. He was also cut around the eyes by then, but staged such a courageous revival that Canzoneri, who had world title experience in 23 fights at bantam, feather, light and light welter weights, only just shaded it.

Berg went on fighting, and usually winning, in America until his return to Britain in 1934 with almost 120 fights behind him. Although he was still young there was a theory that he might be burnt out, over the hill, past it, not as dangerous. Berg was to show the sceptics what they

This was typical of Berg in action, scorning defence to flail away two-fisted at Louis Saerens.

could do with their theories. By the end of the year he had taken the British lightweight championship from a very useful stylist and correct puncher, Harry Mizler. The story goes that Mizler was made a mite apprehensive by the menacing fury of the way Berg warmed up in the dressing room they shared. It is possible, but also more valid, that he damaged both hands hitting Berg's head and took so much other punishment doing it that he had to quit in the tenth.

After losing the lightweight title to Jimmy Walsh in 1937 when he twisted ankle ligaments so badly that he could not stand up, Berg still had tilts at America in 1938 and 1939 with enough of the old fire to draw the crowds. Losing only five out of twenty four was not bad, though it was an indication that time was running out. He came back to "do his bit" in the RAF as a Physical Training Instructor and used his leaves lucratively with the odd fight – though the rising stars of the day, such as Ernie Roderick and Arthur Danahar, were too young and quick for him. Still, after almost two war-time years of inaction, at the age of 36 he managed to win all of his last three fights in 1945.

Berg continued to be a familiar figure; lively, articulate and impeccably turned out at ringside for many years. He was honoured with a trophy for services to his sport by the Boxing Writers in 1985 when he was 75. Then the nation was reminded of his story when he received a show-business accolade – a starring part in *This is Your Life*.

DAVE CROWLEY
(1910 — 74)

Dave Crowley, the former British Lightweight Champion and one of England's liveliest and best-loved fighters between 1929 and 1946, had more reason than most boxers to laugh at the celluloid fist-fights so often screened by Hollywood – usually in Westerns. The hero and villains land fifty full-blooded punches to each others' heads without even sucking their knuckles, raising a bruise, taking a count, or bleeding. Dave knew all there was to know about the real thing, which is why he was called in to organise, orchestrate and co-ordinate the most authentic-looking movie punch-up ever seen in British post-war movies, between a returning commando hero, John Mills, and Stewart Grainger, the spiv who had stolen the soldier's girlfriend. That sequence in *Waterloo Road* was so convincing in its realism that Dave Crowley received a special screen credit, and yet, for genuine blazing excitement, action and interest it could not match his own colourful career during an era packed with spectacularly good fighters. In 180 fights he went in 34 times against men who, at some stage of their own careers, were champions. That is as many bouts as some modern fighters amass in a lifetime.

Five of those fights were against world champions at four different weights – flyweight Jackie Brown, bantamweight Panama Al Brown, featherweights Mike Belloise and Petey Sarron, and lightweight Freddie Miller. At the end of it all there was not a mark on an always handsome, cheerful face, nor a stumble in his jaunty, quickstepping stride. He rejoiced in his image as the James Cagney of the ring. The only hint of his profession were twisted, misshapen hands, buckled by the thousands of punches he had thrown.

He had already had more than seventy fights when he had his own first championship chance, in the days before those fragile fists started to hurt almost as much as they hurt his opponent. He very nearly won the British Featherweight title from the great Nel Tarleton at the Albert Hall in December 1934 with one punch, a terrific right, that had the Liverpudlian maestro out on his feet at the end of the fifth round. One

Mirror, mirror on the wall. Crowley, the Jimmy Cagney lookalike, shows a classy stance in shadow-boxing.

more clean hit might have finished him, when the bell went.

Expert work in the corner can sometimes save a man and one of the best, Ted Broadribb, who, when he boxed as "Young Snowball" actually knocked out Georges Carpentier (then aged sixteen), was in Tarleton's. As Broadribb rubbed and massaged his fighter he saw one of Crowley's attendants smearing Vaseline round the challenger's eyes, and said nothing. But as Crowley came bounding out, looking to finish it, the wily Ted held on to Tarleton and yelled a protest at the referee. The official ordered a halt, examined Crowley's face, signalled for a towel and wiped away the offending grease. It all added up to maybe thirty seconds of precious and absolutely vital recovery time and a clear-headed Tarleton won on points.

No one complained. Crowley himself pulled a few gamesmanship strokes of his own in his time and suffered a few more during a 1936 trip to the States, when he boxed a ten-round, non-title draw against World Featherweight Champion Mike Belloise, which most ringsiders thought he had won. No matter, it earned him a re-match, with the title at stake, in September the same year in New York. It was to end in a controversy which saw the British Boxing Board urged to ban fighters under their control from boxing in the States, unless the controversial "no-foul" rule was abandoned. Under those rules, Crowley had been awarded one of the rounds, the fifth, because, after slipping to his knees, Belloise clouted him with a left hook. Under the same rules, referee Arthur Donovan took no notice when the Londoner went down, writhing in pain from a solid punch, claiming a foul. He counted Crowley out in the ninth.

It has to be admitted that Crowley did have a reputation as an actor. He was a notorious groin-grabber who could simulate death throes if an opponent caught him illegally. He actually won ten of his 128 victories by disqualification, but it is doubtful whether he would have tried it on in a world title fight he was clearly leading on points. Again, it did not much matter. Boxing and life were always an enjoyable game to him and in any case he was putting on the weight that made him British Lightweight Champion in May 1938 after an easy points win against Liverpool's Jimmy Walsh at Anfield.

By the following Christmas he was an ex-champion after one of those fights which abide in legend. Crowley really enjoyed most of it, against the ten years younger and vastly less skilful boy wonder, eighteen-year-old Eric Boon. Crowley was on top from the first round, hugely relishing the split-second timing which saw Boon's swings flailing at the empty air from which he had just removed his head. Young Eric's left eye was swelling by the end of that first round. In the sixth it was cut. By the seventh it was just a slit, buried beneath a plum-sized bruise. Crowley was taunting and mocking him with the deadly professional purpose of inviting more wild swings to be easily avoided. Those who know, will confirm that missing is far more tiring than landing. Crowley was slithering in and out, piling up points with fists that were starting to hurt – though even the incredibly strong young Boon did wobble briefly from a right in the ninth.

But the Crowley game plan was not working. Battered, bruised and half-blind, Boon was as full as ever of spite and fight and it was Crowley who went down in the twelfth from a right to the body, claiming, almost inevitably, a low punch. The referee, the stern C.B. Thomas, ignored him, started counting – and Crowley was up as sparky as ever to outbox Boon for the rest of that round and all through the twelfth. But, with his hands hurting and his heart sickened, he walked into a full-blooded right to the chin in the thirteenth and all the good work he had done before was wasted when, instead of speedily retreating, he went into a ferocious counter-attack. Two punches, left hook, right cross, both to the chin, dropped him unconscious, his head dangling over the bottom rope. He was still lying there when Boon's supporters invaded the ring.

A different war had already broken out when they met in a return at

Harringay in December 1939. It was blossoming nicely into another classic, with Crowley hurt by a left hook in the second round but boxing back so splendidly that he was clearly ahead, when a freak accident finished it in the seventh. Dave had been having Achilles tendon trouble and, spinning out of a clinch, he put all his off-balance weight on a leg that crumpled under him. The tendon had snapped and he had to be carried out of the ring.

He had more than fifty fights during and just after the war, remaining a top attraction against the top men, many of them champions. But towards the end only his boxing brilliance was getting him through against the handicaps of increasingly bad eyesight and crippled hands. In his last fight, against Billy Biddles of Hull at Manor Place Baths, an accidental thumb in the left eye in an eight-rounds points defeat, against a man not remotely in his class, rendered him totally blind on that side. But he remained a jaunty, dapper, proud figure round the ringsides before, in the fifties and sixties, owning and running an immensely popular "pub", "Dave's Bar", in the poshest part of Rome's Via Veneto. (His mother was Italian and he hailed from London's Little Italy, Clerkenwell.)

Before his death, from a heart attack, he was back in London and was a familiar figure giving lessons to the amateur youngsters at the Gainsford Club. He would cheerfully, in his sixties, get in the ring to spar – and those strong, eager lads could not lay a glove on him.

Crowley made Eric Boon miss so many times, but the most important punch still cost him his British title.

ERIC BOON
(1919 — 81)

ARTHUR DANAHAR
(1919 —   )

The stories of Eric Boon and Arthur Danahar belong together because, although they were two very different fighters from contrasting backgrounds with dramatically opposite styles, they became linked together, forever, in boxing history by fourteen rounds of a fight that has gone down into legend. The late Peter Wilson, another legend as *Daily Mirror* sports columnist, who was at ringside for more top class fights over more years in more countries than almost anyone, always maintained that their meeting in Harringay in February 1939 was the greatest spectacle he ever saw two Englishmen provide. Although he wrote colourful extravagant prose, he was always coldly dispassionate when it came to that sort of judicial pronouncement.

Of the two men, Boon was indisputably the greater, arguably the hardest single puncher of all time in his division. He hit like a middleweight and was perhaps the most physically perfectly developed lightweight British boxing has known. Again, like so many others, it was at a blacksmith's anvil in his Cambridgeshire village of Chatteris that his frame was forged. He looked like a scaled down Mr Universe though there was nothing muscle-bound about him when he weaved into menacing action. He started knocking men over early, in the booths and small halls of his native county, travelling between venues on his trusty old bicycle. And this was how he set off on the 70 mile journey to London, to fight for the promoter – who very quickly saw the enormous potential in the handsome curly-haired country lad – Jack Solomons, who very quickly became his manager and transformed him into the "Golden Boy of British Boxing". Jack supplied the publicity in their partnership, Boon the punches.

A few years earlier than their 1935 meeting, Solomons had taken over a derelict church hall in the East End, giving it an aristocratic polish

Boon, the winner, is unable to see out of one eye and Danahar is left wondering how much longer it could have lasted.

by renaming it "The Devonshire Club". Boon made spectacular progress under a shrewd, successful manager but there were outraged protests that he was being rushed to his doom when Solomons matched him in May 1938 against the reigning British Lightweight Champion, Jack Walsh of Liverpool, for an open-air, non-title fight in a Chatteris field.

Boon was seventeen. Walsh was twenty five, in his prime, and had taken the title two years earlier from the great Jack "Kid" Berg, admittedly when the Whitechapel Whirlwind was on the other side of the hill and sliding. All the gloom and disaster merchants were silenced when "Boy" Boon, as he was by then known, won convincingly on points. Plans for a more significant return match had to be shelved when Walsh lost his titles to Dave Crowley and it was against this much tougher new champion that Boon won his title. He became the British Lightweight Champion and the biggest single attraction in the sport a fortnight before his nineteenth birthday with a thirteenth-round knock-out. In earlier times the history of British boxing had been studded with examples of the amazing precocity of young Englishmen, but most of them had performed so much earlier that their successes were shrouded in myth. Boon was the first of the modern breed to become so successful so young.

Coming along steadily at the same time, though by a very different route, was another nineteen year old, Arthur Danahar, a Stepney boy, a real cockney, who had been a brilliant ABA champion in 1939. He had built a string of fourteen successful wins and attracted a huge and growing army of supporters. Most of his fights had been National Sporting Club promotions at The Empress Hall and this helped to add spice to the prospect of a meeting with Boon. Danahar was brought up in the tradition of orthodoxy, a waspish left jab, a crisp and damaging right, twinkling footwork, a good defence – all the so-called English virtues his fans felt would put into perspective the crude and clumsy "take two, land one" assaults of the Champion.

No fight in England before or since has aroused such intense public interest. Harringay's 11,500 seats were sold within a few days of the announcement – and could have been sold three times over. Television, then in its infancy, grabbed at the chance to broadcast it to the few rich customers who considered this unlikely form of entertainment was worth installing in their homes. Three big London cinemas also sold out at inflated prices for special transmissions. Getting a Cup Final ticket was easy in comparison and, in fact, the only reason it was not held over to become an even bigger summertime open-air attraction was that Danahar, as he grew in stature, was also gradually increasing in weight. What was to make the event all the more remarkable, however, was that the fight itself actually lived up to the attention-compelling build-up.

Danahar fans were exchanging delighted "I told you so's" all through the first seven rounds as Boon, four inches shorter at only 5 feet 4 inches, made that disparity all the more obvious by crouching as he prowled forward. Danahar picked him off relentlessly with a left jab straight as a spear, mercilessly accurate.

The flesh around Boon's eye was swelling ominously by the eighth, but even more ominous for his opponent was the eager gleam in his eyes and the grin on his face. Eight rounds was as far as Danahar had ever gone in fourteen contests. Boon had already had 67 fights up to and including championship distance. His own fight was only just beginning and the hooks to the head that dropped Danahar twice in this eighth round were his way of signalling that.

There was no despair – yet – nor was there need for any. Danahar had been well schooled to stay on one knee, take a rest, look at his corner and get up at nine, still composed, his defence and reflexes intact. He was still in the fight as he proved in the ninth and tenth. Boon, his blood up, full of aggression and adrenalin, came charging in and actually went down in each of those rounds, scorning his own chances of a breather. In the eleventh Boon went in for the kill, ignoring the lefts that were still

Boon ducks and backs away from this jab.

Danahar is finding the range this time.

Danahar blocks Boon's hook with a glove.

The end is in sight as Danahar goes down.

bouncing off his head and it is doubtful whether Danahar would have been able to beat the count after being dropped just before the end of the round. The bell did that for him – though under today's more merciful rules the count would have been continued. It is arguable that Danahar's early lead had already been wiped out, but Boon, by the twelfth, had only one eye and Danahar was still pecking away and picking up points. The left glove was a powder-puff by then, however, and Boon simply waded through it to smash him down twice in the round, three times in the thirteenth. Referee Barrington Dalby stopped it when Danahar went down for the ninth time in the fourteenth round.

Few could have recovered from the sort of beating Danahar's courage had caused him to take – he was still trying to get back up when it ended – yet later that same year he grew naturally into welterweight and still retained the class to outpoint, over ten rounds, a very good reigning welterweight champion, Ernie Roderick. In 1941, with the title at stake, it was different and pure sportsmanship possibly cost Danahar the title. Floored early on by a low blow, he insisted it was accidental, refused to stay down and went on to be clearly outpointed.

Boon continued as a vastly popular and successful lightweight, though the war years robbed him of a fortune, until he dropped his title in 1944 to Ronnie James of Wales and also moved up a weight. He always played down the horrific effect of a motor-cycle accident when, without a crash helmet, he collided on a country lane and fractured his skull.

Few people remember that there was a return Boon–Danahar fight at welterweight in the first major promotion of the post-war boxing boom when Jack Solomons, now self-styled "Mr Boxing" as a promoter, staged it as chief supporting contest to the World Light Heavyweight title bout between Freddie Mills and Gus Lesnevich at The White City. It is not surprising that few remembered it – it was distinctly forgettable and that is unsurprising also. Boon remembered how damaging Danahar's left hand had been last time around. Danahar remembered how punishing Boon's hooks had been in counter-attack and was reluctant to lead. For four rounds they did little more than circle, spar for openings and look at each other. In the fifth, when they did start to fight, Danahar went down but, on getting up, floored Boon with what looked like a low punch. The referee did not agree and counted him out.

It was billed as an eliminator for a title fight with Roderick but, in fact, Danahar never got another crack at it. Within a year the chest complaint from which he was already suffering ended his career. When last heard of he was living in retirement in Spain, and no fighter more deserved to enjoy some sunshine.

Boon did fight Roderick unsuccessfully for the title over fifteen

Danahar's career was overtaken by World War II when the only sparring he could get was against fellow Irish Guards.

rounds in December 1948 though, typically, he had the champion hurt and hanging on at the end. And he was to have one last great hurrah the following year. His fight against European champion, Robert Villemain, conqueror of Roderick and an authentic world-class fighter was another epic in the Danahar class – but with a different ending. Ten non-stop rounds of furious action finished with Boon only just failing to beat the count with five seconds remaining of the final round. Had he done so, he had thrown enough punches, done enough damage to have deserved at least a draw. He was only 28 years young at the time, but he was 122 fights old. It was time to call it a day.

DAVE CHARNLEY
(1935 —   )

There was always something chilly and dispassionate about the look in the eyes of Dave Charnley, the undefeated British and European Lightweight Champion. It was direct, disconcerting, maybe even contemptuous. One personal close-range experience may seem insignificant, but it has been remembered over the years.

It was after his victory in April 1958 over another considerable fighter, Peter Waterman, who promptly retired as unbeaten British and European Welterweight Champion at the age of 24 after only his third defeat in 46 contests. He was subdued and stopped in less than five rounds by a smaller but much stronger, more muscular and punishing man. Charnley lay in a bath soaking a body that was also tired and aching – because although comprehensively beaten, Waterman was too proud a fighter, too good a puncher not to have managed to land plenty of his own rib-bending hooks. As a conventional convenient post-fight commencement to a conversation, a fairly meaningless "Good fight, Dave" was offered. He looked at the speaker silently for several seconds before saying, "There's no such thing as a good fight".

He could not have meant he did not like the boxing game. No one could surely have fought with the murderous efficiency he produced even in very occasional defeats if that had been the case. He never showed any reluctance to dish out punishment and never flinched from the necessity of taking it. Although he never won a world title at lightweight he came desperately close to it and was certainly by a distance the best British fighter of modern times to fail. He always had the aura of someone special, outside the ring as well as in it.

Maybe even then he realised that boxing was just one necessary, though important, part of his life, worth the determination, dedication and ability he brought to it, but nevertheless only a part. The reason why he apparently never brooded about going all the way to a lucrative world title was perhaps explained on the night he contacted the hotel which was staging the annual British Boxing Writers Club dinner to explain

*Charnley sways back to draw a right-hand punch from Willie Toweel and is
perfectly positioned to counter.*

why he could not attend. He was talking on the telephone in his new
Rolls Royce, delayed by one of the property deals that made him a
millionaire. It was something else that made him a bit different.

So was his southpaw style, right fist and right foot forward, often an
abomination to orthodox boxers – though few would go as far as Henry
Cooper once did and maintain, "They should be strangled at birth".
Henry was talking in rueful amusement after a meeting with one of the
clumsiest and most awkward southpaws of all time, big Jack Bodell,
having had his toes trampled, his shins bruised and nursing knuckles that
ached after hitting elbows. Too often watching a southpaw is as
unpleasing as fighting one. Watching Dave Charnley was always
worthwhile though fighting him was nobody's idea of fun. His action was
so smooth it was usually the other guy who was to look awkward and
clumsy, inept and unbalanced.

Charnley came into the game after a sparkling amateur career as a
teenager and lost only one of his first eighteen fights to a cagey, more
experienced Frenchman, Guy Gracia, the sort Charnley did not enjoy
fighting because he came more to frustrate than fight. The nineteenth
fight was special, against Sammy McCarthy who had lost the British
featherweight championship a year earlier and had moved up a weight
division at the age of 24. "Smiling Sammy" the boxing writers called him
because, astonishingly, he boxed with a shy grin flickering on a choir-boy
face. He was immensely popular with London crowds who loved his
stinging, accurate left jabs, his sportsmanship and bravery, and he

nurtured ambitions towards the lightweight championship for which Charnley had to wait eight months before becoming eligible at 21.

Charnley smashed him down for nine in the second round, eight in the third with the jabbing rights and crushing lefts that were his trade mark, removing the smile from Sammy before the more experienced man's impeccable orthodoxy got him back into the fight that was decided punch for punch, toe to toe, with Charnley always just a bit harder and faster. From then on Charnley was a destroyer of dreams for every fighter in Britain and Europe. He won the British title from another distinctly useful southpaw, Joe Lucy, in 1957 and held it undefeated for six years. He won the European title in 1960 from Mario Vecchiato of Italy until he relinquished it, again undefeated. It took the best from outside to beat him. The American Carlos Ortiz, who was to become world champion did it. So did the enormously talented South African Willie Toweel, who narrowly outpointed him over fifteen rounds for the Empire title. Charnley had to wait almost two years to get it back, knocking out his opponent with crushing left hooks in the tenth.

Being champion of half the world gave him the right to fight the man who rightly ruled the whole planet. In December 1959 Charnley went to Houston, Texas, to fight the great Joe Brown, the lean mean 33 year old who rejoiced in his self-imposed derisive nickname, "Old Bones". It was one of the few occasions Charnley ever boxed inadequately – or was made to. He had hardly got his act together when he was so badly cut by a clash of heads in the fifth that he was forced to retire – and it rankled.

Just over sixteen months later they met again and the situation was vastly different this time in London. Charnley dominated the second half of the fight, punished Brown and had him close to the cliff edge of exhaustion. Many thought he had won but referee Tommy Little, a brave and honest man, decided he had not wiped out the lead Brown's deadly accurate jabbing had piled up earlier. By the time they met for a third fight in 1963 in Manchester, Brown was 36 and had lost his title to Carlos Ortiz. But that must not completely diminish the style of Charnley's victory – one of cold-eyed ferocity, ending with the savage body punishment that knocked out a man who claimed he had never previously been on the floor. Brown, incidentally, went on boxing at or near the top class for another seven years.

The best British and European lightweights could not live with Dave as he illustrated with the fight that won him a Lonsdale belt and almost all the fifteen rounds against challenger Maurice Cullen in May 1963. The best welterweights in the world were, however, a bit too much and a points defeat by one of the greats, Emile Griffith, who once ruled the world's middleweights, convinced him in his 30th year to quit.

Emile Griffith proved he was a great World Champion by cutting and stopping Charnley, but he had his own bruises to count afterwards.

Many good judges thought Charnley should have taken Joe Brown's world title, but the referee scored the American the winner.

NEL TARLETON
(1906 — 1956)

Merseyside is a place that has known more than its share of sporting heroes, most of them in recent years at Anfield, home of Liverpool Football Club. But even Kevin Keegan, Kenny Dalglish or Ian Rush could never have filled that arena on their own. There was one man who could and did pack it with devotees who turned up in their thousands to support, marvel at and cheer him alone. He was the featherweight known as "Nella", an affectionate adaptation of his name, Nel Tarleton. Bravery is a theme that threads throughout the history of boxing and they never came any braver than this one, who is always right up there when they argue about the great men of his division, alongside Jim Driscoll and Howard Winstone.

The story goes that he was named after Admiral Lord Nelson and, to stretch the coincidence to its ultimate, where the great sailor fought with only one eye, Nella did so, even more remarkably, with only one lung, the legacy of tuberculosis as an infant. Yet he fought professionally and successfully for twenty years from the Depression days of the mid-twenties until 1945 when he ended his career, defending his title successfully to become the first man in his division to win two Lonsdale belts. Pale and frail and skinny, already battling against the lung disease that was to end his life ten years later, he outpointed a man fifteen years younger, the famous Aldgate Tiger Al Phillips.

There were many factors which contributed to the brilliance and the length of his career, 143 fights, still astonishing in view of all his handicaps. One was obviously an aptitude that came to him naturally. One was defensive capability. His hair was groomed into a rather old-fashioned centre parting, Edwardian style, and usually every hair was still in place when the final bell went. He knew all about "rope-a-dope" long before Muhammad Ali invented the technique of going back into the ropes and using their yield to avoid punches by millimetres or absorb their effects by leaning back into them, sometimes catapulting off them waspishly. At the end of his career the most obvious scars on his body

One of Tarleton's own favourite photographs, used in the programme on the night he fought Panama Al Brown.

were the evidence of old rope burns.

Another factor was an almost uncanny ability to pace a fight so perfectly to last the distance throughout his career - he was never knocked out or stopped - though occasionally there were only a few drops of fuel left in the tank. The only thing he ever lacked was a chilling knock-out punch. Only twelve of his opponents were counted out,

*Johnny King of Manchester, left, sways away from this Tarleton attack,
but his challenge for the title was unsuccessful.*

*Tarleton throws a right that is almost too fast for the camera to catch, but
King is safely out of range.*

*An indication of Tarleton's height and reach disadvantage against the
World Bantamweight Champion, the 6 foot Brown.*

*Johnny Cuthbert goes down briefly, but got up to lose the British
Featherweight title to Tarleton.*

Tarleton's favourite trick, swaying back into the ropes to stay out of trouble as World Champion Miller charges in.

although another 29 were rescued by referees after an accumulation of punishment, or retired hurt – and bewildered by his humming-bird speed.

Amongst the most memorable of his fights were two of the eight that were drawn – and both were against men who held world titles. The first was in 1932 against the freakish Panama Al Brown. He stood an inch under 6 feet tall, although he was the reigning World Champion at bantamweight, weighing 8 stone 6 lbs. With his arms outstretched, finger tip to finger tip he measured 76 inches. He towered over Tarleton, reckoned slightly above average height himself. A colourful saying in American sportswriting – "You've gotta dance with the one that brought ya", it translates as "You must stick to the style that has won you success" – had to be ignored by Nella that night at Anfield. Instead of jabbing he had to let Brown do the leading, try to get under a left arm as long as a spear, hook away to the body and slither out of trouble again. Tarleton always thought he did it often enough to win.

The following year, 1933, on a four months tour to Australia he had what he always maintained was his hardest fight, against Tod Morgan, an American who had held the World Junior Lightweight title for four years at the end of the twenties. He was a full stone heavier than the skinny, narrow-chested Tarleton and, at thirty, he was far from finished. Morgan, in fact, had another 60 fights in the next eight years. Tarleton only just beat the count in the first round from a booming right and was bounced up and down by the stronger, heavier man for four rounds so one-sided it would probably have been stopped in today's more merciful climate. Morgan put so much effort into trying to finish it that he punched himself out. Gradually Tarleton's impeccable boxing piled up enough points for most ringsiders to believe he had won. He did not dispute this particular verdict, however. "At one point I'd have been glad to come out of it alive", was the way his Scouse humour saw it.

His own choice as the outstanding performance of his career was his second challenge for the World Featherweight title in 1934 against the great American southpaw Freddie Miller, who had outpointed him the previous year. Nel Tarleton had never lost a return fight in his life – because lessons learned were always carefully stored away in the memory bank of a marvellous boxing brain. Although he was knocked down early in the first round, Tarleton came back fighting so furiously throughout the rest of it that he was convinced he deserved the decision. But British referees have always had a reputation for giving foreigners a fair deal and traditionally were reluctant to take a title from a champion after a close fight. Jack Smith, the Harry Gibbs of his day, lifted the American's arm.

Tarleton felt bitter enough to contemplate, unthinkably, quitting the game and in fact came close to doing that after an off-form night in September 1936, when he dropped his British title to the tough, clever Glaswegian, Johnny McGrory. In fact, he had only seven more fights in the following four years, with illness and a bad accident that wrecked his right knee contributing to inactivity. Yet in the seventh of those fights the title that McGrory had relinquished was regained from Johnny Cusick, the first notch on that second Lonsdale belt. Beating Tom Smith in the same year, 1940, brought him within one defence of making it his own.

No one gave him much chance of achieving it in February 1945 at Belle Vue, particularly when, after being hustled and bustled and trailing on points against Al Phillips, he had to hang on desperately to avoid a knock-out in the tenth after a solid right to the jaw. Yet incredibly he dredged up last reserves of skill, stamina and sheer ringcraft to win the next five rounds – and keep both the belt and the title.

PAT COWDELL
(1 9 5 3 —   )

There was one very good reason why Pat Cowdell, the British Featherweight Champion, from Warley in the Midlands, was the only person in the huge inhibiting Astrodome, in Houston, Texas, on the night of 12 December 1981 who seemed supremely unconcerned about his own physical safety. He was armoured by his own unshakeable certainty of how much he knew, how much he had learned about looking after himself in boxing rings in many countries in his 28 years.

But for the rest of the boxing fraternity there was still considerable concern about the damage that seemed likely to be done by the 22-year-old he was challenging. At the time, Salvador Sanchez of Mexico was on his way to being recognised as the greatest champion in the history of his division. Before he was killed in a car crash eight months later he had defended his title nine times, three of them against men who were good enough to become champions themselves once he had gone - Azumah Nelson, Wilfredo Gomez, Juan Laporte.

None of them performed with greater skill and courage than Pat Cowdell did that night. He was nobility in boxing gloves and when the hardest punch of the fight, a long looping right, dropped him for nine towards the end of the fifteenth, even the Mexican fans in the crowd wanted him to last the distance, to be able to tell his grandchildren he had gone all the way with the very best in the business. For more than half the fight he actually did rather more than that, boxing out of a familiar crouch, his chin tucked out of sight and outjabbing the uncomfortable Sanchez. The champion even turned southpaw for a spell, not knowing Cowdell had dealt accurately with plenty of wrong-way-round fighters. Cowdell was in front on points until the ninth, when a wicked left hook ripped open his right eyebrow. From then on he was taken apart.

Everyone except one judge, a Texan, knew there was only one winner - he scored it to Cowdell by one round. The honest and sporting Cowdell - characteristics he showed throughout his career - put that official in his place when he said, "Sanchez is a great champion who hurt me more than anyone has ever done. If they had asked me after the fight to be one of the judges I would still have given it to Sanchez."

Pat knew all about the eccentricities, stupidities and sometimes rank criminal bias of judges from personal experience during a long distinguished amateur career of something like 300 contests. Unlike so many professionals, an ABA title for him was not just a stepping stone to the punch-for-pay game. He won four of them, at bantamweight and lightweight and two at featherweight, as well as National Boys Club and Junior ABA titles. He won Commonwealth Gold, European Bronze, represented England innumerable times, and it was only a dreadful judging decision during the 1976 Montreal Olympics that prompted his decision to turn pro the following year. He knew he could, perhaps should, have won the gold medal after outboxing and knocking down in the third round a North Korean, Yong Jo Gu, who went on to take the big prize. Cowdell was so upset by what appeared to be politically inspired judging that, before he was persuaded to change his mind, he threatened to fly straight home and take no part in the awards ceremony that gave him a comparatively meaningless bronze.

At the age of 24, Cowdell, with his smooth, slippery style, was a seasoned fighter before he turned professional, and by his twelfth paid fight was ready for Dave Needham's title. A points verdict went against him very controversially, but brought a return within a couple of

Jimmy Flint was a tremendous puncher, but it was Cowdell who did all the scoring to keep his British title.

months, in November 1979, at the Albert Hall and this time there could be no arguments. Cowdell's crisp punching picked off the aggressive Needham throughout the fight. To prove the point he took only twelve rounds to do it again the following year.

In between came the fight that made Cowdell recognised as the undisputed, absolute master of any British featherweights of the time – a victory over Jimmy Flint, one of those men blessed with a natural asset Cowdell never had, a genuine, chilling knock-out punch. It was worth the big – for those days – purse Mike Barrett paid and the equally large, for the time, twenty guineas ringside prices he charged. Flint's six fights the previous year had lasted less than a total of eighteen rounds and, although the Londoner had never boxed more than eight rounds, he was like all Terry Lawless fighters, as fit as a butcher's dog. The thrill that sold the tickets – what would happen when Flint caught up with the champion? – was answered conclusively. When it happened in the ninth, with Cowdell so far in front he was almost out of sight, Pat took it, shook it off and came back with a two-fisted battering so one-sided that the ever compassionate Lawless retired his man at the end of the eleventh.

After his 1981 epic against Sanchez, Cowdell returned, with ability unimpaired and fitness intact, to go prospecting on the Continent, successfully enough to win and defend the European title, but at the age of 29 decided to retire for what at the time seemed the best of all possible motives. Even though he would have earned £15,000 from a proposed defence against a French nonentity called Von Tripp, Cowdell resisted the lure of money for a softer option. Training, roadwork, gymnasiums and sparring had denied him much family life with his wife and children. He thought he craved it.

Throughout his youth he had passed up another aspect of what some consider part of life's rich pattern. Lads he grew up with were going out for a few drinks and a good time. Denied by a strict boxing regimen, Cowdell wanted a bit of that too – but it very swiftly palled. "I tried it for a while and soon found it could be more damaging to your body and your brain than boxing ever could," he said. Boxing, at the level to which his skill had taken him, was a safe sport, he insisted.

Besides, he actually missed the glow of well-being that physical fitness gave him and there was the attraction of a new weight division, Junior Lightweight, at which he won the European title within a few months of his return to the ring at the age of 31, after a year and a half away. He did decide privately to retire again – although he kept it quiet this time and changed his mind – after he had tried to move back down to featherweight, tempted by another world title fight when he was sensationally knocked out in a single round by the big-punching

Each time Pat Cowdell fought Dave Needham he improved steadily and in their third title fight the referee had to stop it in twelve.

Ghanaian Azumah Nelson. His pride was badly dented that night and even his own most fervent Birmingham fans begged him to quit seven months later after another one-round knock-out by the wild-swinging Morroccan-born Mancunian, Najib Daho. Cowdell felt in his heart that he had simply been uncharacteristically careless and caught cold by crude punches he should have evaded with consummate ease. "I knew it was still there," he maintains and proved it by regaining the title from Daho with a comprehensive display of skills in a one-sided win. "I always intended to go out at the top and what was encouraging me was retaining my enthusiasm for training."

"When you've been in boxing a long time that is the hardest part. Ability is obviously important but the crucial factors for a long career in this game are condition and dedication. I tell my children to put everything into whatever they do. They can see from videos of my fights just what their old man managed to achieve by doing that. And also what he was prepared to go through to achieve it. It was never simply for the money. I just loved being a boxer."

He knew, in May 1988, at the age of 35, however, that it was definitely time to pack up, when the very useful up-and-coming Welshman Floyd Havard took his title from him. Cowdell outfoxed as much as outboxed the youngster for half a dozen rounds, but the legs started to go in the seventh and referee Larry O'Connell stopped it in the eighth round.

JOE BOWKER

(1883 — 1955)

Joe Bowker, who was to become World Bantamweight Champion and retire rich for his times, was desperate when the postman arrived at his tiny house in a Salford slum with a letter from the man who was then the most powerful figure in boxing, Mr A.F. "Peggy" Bettinson, founder and autocratic ruler of the National Sporting Club in London. It requested a seventeen year old who had already won a string of local fights - and many more in the boxing booths - to come at once to take part in a novices competition. This was the boxing equivalent of a Royal Command and the reason for Bowker's desperation was simple poverty. Trains were too expensive. He could not afford to buy a bicycle. Hitch-hiking had not even been heard of at the turn of the century - there were no cars and not all that many roads made up - so he took the advice of Sherlock Holmes: "When there is only one alternative left, that is the solution." He walked almost two hundred miles to London, living and sleeping rough.

Ten days later he arrived at Bettinson's office to be rebuked sharply, "I thought I told you to come at once." Bowker explained meekly, "I walked as quick as I could, sir", and that tickled the man Bowker always referred to later as "The Guv'nor". Bettinson was even more pleased when Bowker showed his enormous potential by winning five fights in a single night to take first prize in that novices competition in what was for him, in those days, a totally alien environment.

There has never been any boxing venue quite like the National Sporting Club in Covent Garden. The ring was situated in the centre of a basement theatre under a massive chandelier. The more distinguished of the members-only patrons, usually dinner-jacketed, sat on stage, while other spectators took their places in the stalls - after they had all extravagently eaten and drunk in the dining room upstairs. A Master of Ceremonies strictly enforced silence during the rounds. Boxers were firmly instructed to "try to overcome your adversary in a fair, manly and sporting spirit and bear in mind that there is more honour in losing like a gentleman than winning like a blackguard". They took to little Joe Bowker immediately, which is why he remained a favourite for a full nineteen years. They loved the brilliance of his boxing, the way he could keep his handsome head out of an opponent's reach, sometimes for twenty rounds, all the time collecting points for a connoisseur to savour.

Bowker was still a month away from his nineteenth birthday when he did that to take the British Bantamweight title from a very capable champion, Harry Ware, in June 1902 – but had a back-to-earth shock when he went round to "The Guv'nor's" office next morning. Bettinson, himself a former British Amateur Lightweight Champion, told him, "You won and did well, deserved it, but you made about fifty mistakes." He then removed his jacket, told Bowker to do the same, cleared furniture out of the way and showed the new champion gaps he had left in his guard, openings he had failed to take.

It is hard to imagine many modern-day promoters who could do that – though Micky Duff was a slippery customer in his own boxing day. It is even more difficult to picture the reaction of some of today's more disdainful champions. Bowker saw it as sound advice and, not for the first time in his career, went back to the travelling boxing booths for a spell. He found putting on the gloves with any man who fancied his chances an improvement on sparring because he took on challengers of all sizes, shapes and styles – and besides he was getting paid and not getting hurt. He developed into a marvel of quickness and cunning in a series against the best men around until he was pronounced ready for an American who must rate as one of history's most confident – or overconfident – world champions.

Frankie Neil, almost exactly the same age as Bowker, was a complete contrast. He had tremendous punching power, which Bowker lacked, in both hands and had knocked out the vast majority of his opponents. A built-in swagger that was part of his nature prompted him to suggest a £1,000 side-stake. Bettinson agreed with a histrionic reluctance that concealed private glee, so Neil pushed the deal one stage further by suggesting the winner should take all the prize money. "That's all right, Guv'nor," said the unperturbed Bowker.

He was always a conscientious trainer, but the little man had never been in better shape than he was that night of 17 October 1904 at the NSC. Neil had not come to box; his plan was to smash, batter, overwhelm Bowker and for several rounds it seemed as though this might happen. The Englishman was hurtling around the ring like a leaf in a gale, but it gradually dawned on the enthralled members that not many of the storm of American hailstones were actually landing. Bowker was at his very best, which was magical, as his dazzling skill rendered all that power impotent and by half-way through the fight he was already well in front and drawing away. The artist went on steadily scoring against the strong man until by the twentieth Bowker had won by a mountain of points. Neil's camp had to cancel the victory dinner they had already booked at the Café Royal and Bettinson is said to have generously chipped in to help pay the fares back to San Francisco.

At 21 Joe was growing into the featherweight division with considerable success. In an outstanding fight he virtually ended the career of one of the greats, "Pedlar" Palmer, several inches taller and pounds heavier. Palmer was reckoned one of the most clever, tricky and slippery boxers of the age, but Bowker outclassed him, knocking him down three times before the fight was stopped in the twelfth.

One of the truly all-time great featherweights, Peerless Jim Driscoll, the legendary Welshman, was in his prime at the time, but in May 1906 Bowker, six pounds lighter and not in serious training, agreed to come in as substitute against him. Driscoll's points win over fifteen rounds convinced Bowker that over the championship distance and fully fit he would do better. He was wrong. This time Driscoll's advantages in height and reach were even more decisive and Bowker was stopped in the seventeenth.

He came to grief again against the enormous hitting power of the man who was to finish Driscoll's career, Charles Ledoux of France – through a moment of flashy carelessness that was absolutely untypical. In the eighth round Bowker, by then convinced he was far too clever for a dangerous opponent, turned his head away to wink confidently at his corner. A tremendous right to the jaw caught him. He was knocked down six times in the ninth and five more times in the tenth before the referee stopped it.

Bowker was to carry on fighting and winning and invariably delighting audiences with his artistry until well after World War I and continued to give something back to boxing as trainer of Great Britain's Olympic team. In between he had lost his bantamweight crown to Digger Stanley, but that is another story, a different chapter that belongs to another man, the winner.

*Joe Bowker, passing on his knowledge to Britain's team before the Berlin
Olympics, lifted the tension by acting as a human golf tee during training.*

GEORGE "DIGGER" STANLEY
(1883 — 1919)

George "Digger" Stanley, one of the most colourful, controversial and, it has to be faced, arguably the dirtiest little fighter of his era, is reported variously to have been born in a gypsy caravan at places as wide apart as Norwich and Kingston upon Thames. Perhaps his mother was on the move at the time. It never seemed particularly important to a man who could neither read nor write and who, if he ever had the rules of boxing read to him, clearly did not take too much notice. He boxed in an era of great Bantamweight World Championship claimants and won fights against some of the best of them: George Dixon, Jimmy Walsh, Charles Ledoux – and Joe Bowker for the title in October 1910.

Bowker had been fighting as a featherweight and had to boil himself down for the challenge. His face was thin and drawn, every rib was visible through his skin and for Digger Stanley it set the tone of the fight. He made Bowker's kidneys a target for punches, sometimes delivered karate-style with the edge of his hand, trying to weaken and wear down his man. He also wrestled him through the ropes, leaned on him in the clinches, held his man with one hand and hit him with the other. Digger's reasoning was basic. He knew that while he was rated the hardest-hitting bantamweight of his time, Bowker was recognised as something just as important – the hardest to hit. Bowker therefore had to be slowed down until he could be caught.

The fight finished in chaos in the eighth when Digger hammered in a right to the body that sent Bowker down groaning and rolling in agony claiming a foul while he was counted out. The decision was delayed for a medical examination and a ring announcement by "Peggy" Bettinson stated that there was no evidence of a low punch.

Digger Stanley was the new World Bantamweight Champion – and a very good one. He was also enormously popular because outside the ring he was such an engagingly simple and likeable little man. One of his proudest possessions in prosperous days was an expensive gold watch which he would ostentatiously flick open and consult, though the effect

Digger Stanley, never fussy about the rules, traps Bowker's arms and gets in with his head

was ruined when he invariably had to ask someone else to tell the time. He never learned to do that either. He drove to distraction his backer, a wealthy bookmaker, Alf Mack, who had put up the side-stake money for the Bowker fight and was anxious to make a lot more with a trip to the United States to clean up various American claimants to the title. Digger had a couple of hundred pounds in his pocket and was more keen to follow his expensive gypsy love of trotting racing by buying a mare. He pleaded domestic worries and it was only when Mr Mack installed Mrs Stanley in a little grocer's shop that Digger was finally persuaded to board ship in January 1911.

Mr Mack had to listen to and, in the end, become disheartened by constant pleas of "Let's go 'ome Alf. Let's go 'ome please" for months, the first time actually on the rough Transatlantic crossing when an alarmed Digger woke him to ask why the engines had stopped. Alf went off to enquire and reported that the captain had temporarily lost his bearings. "What's them?" asked Stanley and was utterly panic-stricken when told. "You mean 'e don't know where the 'ell 'e is. Oh Alf, let's go 'ome."

He was persuaded into a ten-round no-decision overweight match in New York in February 1911 against Frankie Jones and for at least the thirty minutes of the fight did feel thoroughly at home and comfortable. Jones made the mistake of trying to rough up Digger Stanley and a wry comment of a famous referee, the old Wild West gunman and sheriff, Bat

Masterson, said it all: "Frankie tried out a few tricks and found the Britisher had forgotten more than he had ever learned."

Digger Stanley seemed destined to become an enormous success in the States where they like their fighters rough and ruthless, but a trip to the tough city of Philadelphia where he boxed another no-decision six-rounder against Tommy O'Toole proved disastrous for the enterprise – hilariously. Digger listened wide-eyed to a Philadelphia policeman he met in a pool room telling a tale of how he had shot and killed at least one man during a strike-breaking operation, discovering that all American cops carried guns and were alarmingly ready to use them. He would dive flat in the street if he heard a car backfire and, no prizes for guessing, would sheepishly ask yet again "Let's go 'ome Alf" when he got up. The final straw was when someone read to him a letter from Mrs Stanley complaining that business in the shop was bad. All the bright ambitious plans had to be abandoned.

Back home the fans loved his two successful championship twenty-round defences against Ike Bradley in Liverpool in September 1911 and the Frenchman Charles Ledoux in London in April 1912, with brilliant boxing from Stanley and, surprisingly, quite good behaviour – though a return against Ledoux was a mistake that cost him his world title in June that same year in Dieppe. After surviving a hectic couple of rounds, including a brief knockdown in the first, Digger was convincingly outpointing the big-punching Frenchman when he made his mistake in the seventh. After landing with a goodish stiff right cross, experience should have taught him to step back and examine the effect. Instead, he rushed back into a flurry of punches – one observer reported that at least twenty caught him flush to the head – and he was still unconscious when they carried him to his corner.

One sportswriter of the time wondered whether Digger wanted to be back at his hotel in time for dinner. They always treated his eccentricities and occasionally outrageous illegalities lightly. "He has never quite acclimatised himself to the niceties of the Queensberry code," wrote one.

After another successful defence of his British title against the Scot Alex Rafferty later the same year, it was reported that, "Digger introduced us to a novel and most ingenious use of his left shoulder as Rafferty's bruised mouth will testify. The Digger's lefts might have missed but when they did that trusty shoulder was always ready to fill the gap." Digger Stanley always somehow contrived to make his worst excesses look accidental and always looked appealingly apologetic and contrite. He stole rather than earned forgiveness. He did lose the title temporarily and sensationally in June 1913 to Welshman Bill Beynon, a

Digger could stand up and box elegantly. He could also, if necessary, come in crouching and two fisted.

substitute who had taken off a stone inside a week and started with an injured eye. Ring generalship deserted Digger completely. Instead of outboxing Beynon he tried the rough stuff, was warned a dozen times in a rough house for butting, hitting after the bell, holding and hitting and was outpointed. Still, he did all the right things to regain it six months later.

Digger was finally deposed by a younger man, Curley Walker, in April 1914 when the strictest referee of the day, the famous J.W.H.T. Douglas, tired of too many of his antics and disqualified him in the thirteenth round. It was to become a familiar ending. He went on slowly deteriorating, lost ten of his last sixteen contests up to 1918 and in seven of those, including the last three in a row, was disqualified. At the end he was on crutches after a hip injury and he died penniless a year later. All the money had gone, most of it on the trotting horses he loved to back at odds he could not properly work out. He even achieved his dream at one stage of buying a small string. But typically he did not have enough money or sense to buy a stable and eventually had to hand them over in settlement of their feed and keep. It somehow, sadly, says it all about his carefree, feckless gypsy nature.

TEDDY BALDOCK
(1907 — 71)

Teddy Baldock might never have become Bantamweight Champion of the world if he had succeeded in his first job as an apprentice jockey at Epsom. He was sacked within a fortnight for fighting with – and knocking out – a more promising rider. His distinctly annoyed father promptly encouraged him to turn professional boxer just before his fourteenth birthday. They were hard days.

Baldock senior should have realised earlier that the boy was born to fight. As a useful middleweight himself, he used to go down on his knees in the tiny Poplar house to teach the nipper, christened Alfred but inevitably re-named "Titch". Even as an infant his son managed to bloody his parent's nose – and the noses of all the children in the neighbourhood. One angry mother, whose offspring had been battered, brought him round to complain and gave her own son an outraged clout when she saw the diminutive size of the mite who had done the damage.

Within a couple of those flyweight years, Baldock had become a top favourite at London's Premierland arena where he was billed as "The Mumtaz Mahal of The Ring" – after a speedy two-year-old horse owned by the Aga Khan. The posters always called him Teddy, though his friends still addressed him as Alf. Speed was always one of his assets, particularly with a straight left that was always more than a mere jab. He punched devastatingly with it even when not much more than a child. His long association with the man who managed him to the end, Joe Morris, started with a recommendation from a former British Featherweight Champion, Mike Honeyman, Baldock's early model and idol – though he eventually far outstripped this elegant fancy dan. The partnership lasted because it was based on trust. Joe Morris never took more than one-sixth of the purse money and always banked the rest, so his fighter lived on a pocket-money allowance and, unlike too many, retired "comfortable" financially, though prematurely. Nowadays 25 per cent is normal and a third, sometimes even half, not unknown.

Because record keeping was not an exact science in those days, by the end of 1925, the year of his eighteenth birthday, Baldock claimed about 100 fights, though "only" 40 – more than the career totals of many moderns – are there to be checked. Among the scalps he collected were those of two world title contenders, Ernie Jarvis and Frankie Ash. Ash, in fact, had only recently gone fifteen rounds against Pancho Villa, conqueror of the great Jimmy Wilde, and one edition of the sports's bible, *Boxing*, awarded Baldock the ultimate accolade by enthusing that he shaped like a second Wilde. There are many anecdotes from those early days. One opponent, offered the choice of £3 for the purse money or ten shillings (50p) for every round he lasted, chose wrongly and only earned thirty shillings (£1.50).

Teddy was also developing a wicked right cross. His immaculate boxing and endearing appearance, with a tip-tilted nose that survived all attempts to change its shape, a modest manner and a habit of winning made him so popular with the East End crowds that Premierland could guarantee full houses when he topped the bill. When he graduated to the Albert Hall, fans who could not afford the charabanc and arena ticket used to wait in Poplar's streets to find out how he had got on.

A flyweight title chance never arrived because Elky Clarke, champion at the time, had to pull out through illness and Teddy was growing into a bantamweight. His first defeat, disqualification in nine rounds against Yorkshireman George Nicholson, was never counted as important because Teddy was such a hot favourite. One ringsider had offered £20 to a cigar on an inside-the-distance victory, and Baldock always insisted that the hook which ended it was legitimate.

Against the advice and wishes of his manager, Teddy, then nineteen, insisted on a trip to New York, where occasional low blows made no difference. Joe Morris feared for his well-being but the only difficulty he had was in his lodgings with a German family who, worried by his apparent physical frailty, insisted on trying to build him up with enormous home-cooked meals that made growing into bantamweight a certainty. New York sportswriters affectionately gave him another nickname, "Red", for the auburn tint in his thatch. He was a hit with them, particularly after demolishing a Canadian champion, Arthur De Champlaine, in 63 seconds, including another count of nine. His own highlight of the trip was buying a car and driving to Philadelphia to see Jack Dempsey train and then lose in the famous "long count" second fight against Gene Tunney.

He won eleven and drew one of twelve fights, some against featherweights in New York, which he loved. But he did not fancy Christmas away from home. His best present was the news Joe Morris had waiting for him at Southampton – a chance of a world title fight within a few months if he could first beat young Johnny Brown, brother of the British and European Champion. Brown's handlers had eagerly agreed because they thought Baldock might be weak at the weight. He won by a knock-out in three one-sided rounds and then had literally to be forced out of his paralysing shyness into a ringside meeting with Royalty. The Prince of Wales wanted to shake his hand.

Newspapermen of the day were accustomed to his shyness. Reporters knocking at his door the morning after fights invariably found he had risen early and disappeared for the day.

The World Bantamweight Championship was in disarray at this time. The National Boxing Association of America had decided to nominate one Bud Taylor as Champion. Britain, outraged, believed that another American, Archie Bell, had at least as good a claim and tempted him with an offer of $5,000 to come to London to fight Baldock for their version of the title. Bell was, incidentally, offered the extra inducement by American promoter Tex Rickard in the event of victory over the Englishman, of a crack at an undisputed crown against Bud Taylor, but Baldock could not be treated the same. He was still a fortnight away from his twentieth birthday and in the States they did not allow anyone under 21 to fight fifteen-rounders.

It was a truly epic fight, the American-style hooker against a more classic British boxer, landing three times as often but only half as hard. It did not make the mathematics of scoring the fight difficult, however, with Baldock well in front with only two rounds left. Bell knew he needed a knock-out and Baldock almost made a fatal error. Instead of just staying out of trouble, pride lured him into a punch-up that saw him struggling to hear the final bell –though he was still clearly ahead.

The same sort of totally misplaced pride made him refuse to call off his first defence, five months later, against a tough South African, Willie Smith, when Baldock was still clearly suffering from the after-effects of 'flu. Knocked down in the eighth and reeling around on the receiving end for another seven punishing rounds, it was a minor miracle he lasted to hear the announcement that he was an ex-world champion at the age of twenty.

An injury to his famous left fist, fractured in three places against an opponent's elbow, held him back for a while but, by the time he was 22, he had sorted out the British bantamweight situation and was officially recognised by the newly formed British Boxing Board of Control after knocking out Johnny Brown and outpointing Alf Pattenden. He was convinced he could regain the world title, but exactly one day after his 24th birthday was forced to change his mind by one of the all-time greats

The boyish looks and boxing elegance of Teddy Baldock are both obvious even in a carefully posed training picture.

in that division, Panama Al Brown. Teddy was tall for his weight at 5 feet 6 inches, but Brown towered a full five inches taller and punched two divisions above his weight. Baldock, although fighting half-blind after a left hook grazed his eyeball in the fourth, fought on for another eight painful rounds before referee Owen Moran mercifully stopped it.

With his hands suspect and his eyesight in danger, a twelve-round points defeat by Dick Corbett convinced him it was time to go. He died in 1971 and the title of his autobiography was a fitting epitaph. It was *Lightning Fists*.

ALAN RUDKIN
(1 9 4 1 —   )

If Alan Rudkin, a lively little man from Liverpool, had been boxing in the bad, bloody old days when men fought for titles over twenty rounds, he would undoubtedly have become Bantamweight Champion of the world. More, he would have been the first Englishman to travel abroad and capture a supreme crown since the great Ted "Kid" Lewis achieved it in 1915.

It is almost twenty years since this cheerful, courageous boxer-fighter journeyed to Melbourne, Australia, to take on a very good champion, the Aborigine Lionel Rose. The contrasting picture of the two men during and after the fifteenth round in the Kooyong Tennis Stadium provides the proof. Rose was pinned on the ropes for most of it, his dark eyes sunk in pits of exhaustion and despair, unable to block or avoid the crisp Rudkin hooks that pounded him. At the bell he collapsed on his stool without enough breath left to answer the entreaty of the MC and whisper a few words to an exulting Aussie audience. Rudkin was still up on his toes, looking ready to go again when Rose collapsed from stomach cramps in his dressing room. He could not possibly have continued for another round. As it was it went to a split decision, with one Australian judge voting for Rudkin by a single point while two countrymen, the referee and a second judge, awarded it to Rose. There were no complaints from Rudkin until the scoring of the second judge was announced. He made Rose a winner by *fifteen* points, did not give Rudkin a round and made the ridiculous assertion afterwards that he had counted up all the punches landed by both men in every round.

Yet Rudkin did lose the first five rounds in a row and was badly cut in the third. His job looked all the more hopeless because of the physical contrast. Rose was built more like a welterweight, three inches taller than Rudkin, well muscled with reach advantage also. His bones must have been made of aluminium to look so big and weigh so little. Yet the enormous lead was gradually chipped away. Two-fisted battling aggression against a superb craftsman took the last four rounds.

Rudkin proved himself the very best of a good crop of British bantamweights
when he kept his title with a points win over Johnny Clark.

Three years earlier Rudkin had already experienced the heartbreak of travelling half-way round the world to lose a world title narrowly on points. This time it was in Tokyo against the muscular Japanese, Fighting Harada – eventually deposed by Rose – who actually tried to fight with sticking plasters protecting his suspect eyebrows. Rudkin was done few favours by a Japanese referee who insisted on a mandatory eight count in the first round when the Liverpudlian claimed indignantly he had been wrestled to the floor. It was so close this might even have been the clinching factor in the verdict.

Rudkin hoped desperately that Rose, who announced he would undertake one more defence before moving up to featherweight, would give him another crack. The chance went instead to a fearsome puncher, Ruben Olivares of Mexico, who won as he usually did, with a knock-out, in the fifth round. It was Olivares Rudkin had to face in his third world title fight in December of the same year, 1969, in California. Olivares had built up an awesome streak of fifty knock-outs in 53 fights and the ending of this one was as inevitable as the next beat of a healthy heart. Rudkin was knocked out in two rounds with the wise guys claiming that he should have tried to jab and run for at least ten rounds.

The theory does not bear close examination because, in fact, he was caught and dropped by a looping left hook in the first round when he was trying without success to take the fight to long range. By attempting to get close to the Mexican he hoped to reduce the leverage room available – though Olivares did not need much. Just how ferociously hard the man punched was illustrated in both second-round knock-downs. Each time Rudkin was already on the way down from right handers when two more left hooks caught him before he hit the floor. Rudkin himself was typically chirpy and cheerful about it afterwards. "At least he didn't hurt me and that is absolutely true. I didn't feel the punches, didn't even see them, knew nothing about them until it was all over." It was in character with the professional attitude he showed throughout his career.

The star of Rudkin's stable at the start was a man who would undoubtedly have figured prominently in this book if his career had lasted longer and had included a championship that once seemed an absolute certainty. He was featherweight Frankie Taylor, gold medallist in the European amateur championships at the start of the sixties. He combined good boxing with natural aggression, rated himself a certainty to beat Howard Winstone, and only lost three of 31 fights, one of them to Carlos Teo Cruz who beat Carlos Ortiz to become World Lightweight Champion. An injury in training threatened his eyesight so this 23-year-old apprentice reporter turned full-time sportswriter and is now boxing correspondent of the *Sunday People*. Not that Alan Rudkin would have stayed in anyone's shadow for very long. The first point that struck anyone who met him outside the ring during his career was the astonishing youthfulness of a cherubic choirboy face. Inside the ring a left hook was more likely to strike you. He emerged as top bantamweight in an era which included a crop of enormously talented men. Among them were two former World Flyweight champions who grew out of division – Irishman Johnny Caldwell from whom he won the British title and Scotsman Walter McGowan who took the championship from Alan, then lost it to him again over two terrific fifteen-rounders.

Towards the end of his career he was starting to struggle to shed pounds to make the 8 stone 6 lbs limit, something he cheerfully admitted and which actually suited his manager Bobby Neill just fine. "Alan is at his best when he has to drive himself and sweat in training. It makes him mean," he said when, after an unsuccessful challenge, a points defeat for the British Featherweight Champion against Jimmy Revie in 1970, he came back down again to regain the European title from Franco Zurlo of Italy five months later in eleven rounds which went mainly one way.

But it was getting progressively harder and that was amply illustrated when, after once again proving himself the best of British with his second win over Johnny Clark, he retired to take a pub in his native city. Within a couple of years he could not have made middleweight.

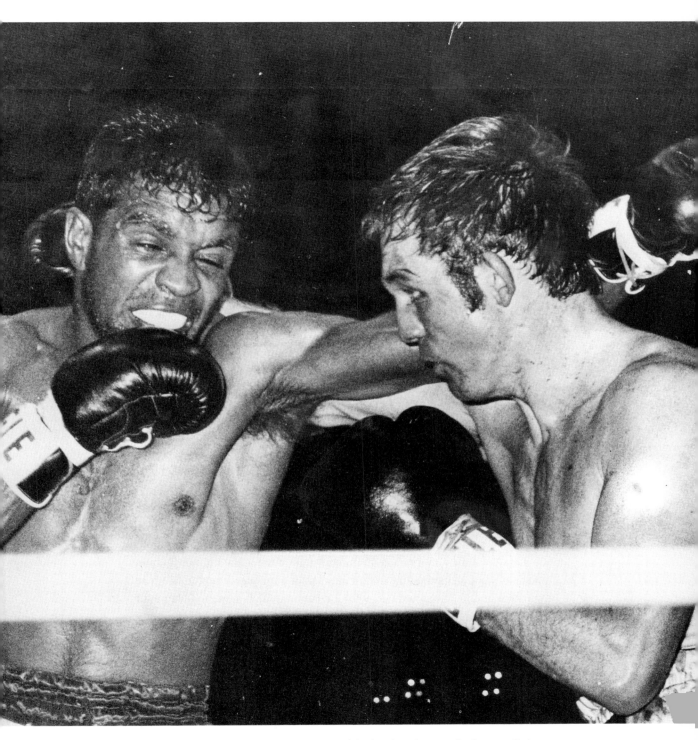

*Rudkin came close to winning a world title when he punched Australia's
Lionel Rose to a standstill in Melbourne.*

JACKIE BROWN
(1909 — 71)

There is nothing which provides boxing's paying customers with more lip-smacking relish than a genuine grudge fight, a meeting of men who just do not like each other. Jackie Brown, of Manchester, who was to become Flyweight Champion of the world, had a whole mini-series of them against Bert Kirby, of Birmingham, the character who at one time disrupted and interrupted his rise to the top.

There is a fascinating story about the fight which propelled both into controversy – their first meeting in a run-down ramshackle former ice rink in West Bromwich, known as The Paradise Street Arena. The promoter, Ted Salmon, had signed Brown, then just a month short of his twentieth birthday, to meet Kirby, the local Midlands favourite, in a final eliminator for the British title in October 1929 and was hoping for not much more than covering the cost of the prize money.

Then the reigning British Champion, Johnny Hill, a Scot, collapsed and died tragically young at 23; Brown v. Kirby was recognised as for the vacant title – and Mr Salmon had a sensational attraction on his hands. Eight thousand customers packed the scruffy arena to the rafters with thousands more locked outside on a Sunday morning that must have affected a few church attendances. For two slum-bred youngsters in those days of the Depression it was the equivalent of two hungry, angry terriers being tossed a bigger bone than either had ever seen. Each went for the jugular from the bell, with Brown so wild he was warned for slapping – though Kirby paid when the Mancunian closed his gloves properly and landed a right uppercut to wipe out some of the advantages Kirby had gained.

Kirby felt that the cut over his left eye that was opened in the second round was caused by a butt, though Brown, always fast and tricky, was outspeeding him and stepped up that pace in the third. This time there was an audible crack of heads as Brown came darting in and Kirby staggered back, his hands down, dazed. Brown pounced to swing another full-force right and Kirby fell straight back flat, striking his head on the boards, unconscious for longer than the necessary ten seconds. The fans, mainly from the Midlands, rioted. Police had to clear the hall and it was several hours before the streets were safe. The British Boxing Board found this particularly unseemly for a Sunday and it was many years later before they allowed another sabbath fight.

With Kirby insisting that Brown was a lucky, dirty little so and so, a return match was inevitable and they were ready for another go at Holborn Stadium in March 1930. There was a smell of sulphur in the air, thick with threats, counter threats and taunts. Alerted by the obvious needle nature of the contest the Board appointed the notoriously strict J.W.H.T. Douglas, known irreverently in his own amateur boxing days as "Johnny Won't Hit Today". Brown and Kirby were both advised by their corners to keep their heads because no sport does more to teach the value of coolness than boxing. The man who goes in wildly swinging through a red mist of rage and hate is easy to pick off and knock out. In fact they went to the other extreme. Referee Douglas had to warn them both for holding and instruct them to get on with it as the crowd started to stir impatiently.

Trying to oblige with more convincing action in the third round, Brown completely missed with a right swing at Kirby that left him half-turned away from his challenger, off-balance, completely exposed. Kirby accepted the invitation with a right of his own that sent Brown into the ropes, then hooked with the left so hard that Brown was left semi-conscious hanging there. The excited Kirby actually missed with his first attempt to finish it, a right uppercut, but steadied himself to land full force with the same hand. It sent Brown clean out of the ring with only his feet hooked over the bottom ropes keeping him from toppling into the ringside seats. He was counted out in that position.

Brown's brooding disappointment grew into seething fury when he was kept waiting for a third "rubber" match. Kirby was in no hurry. He wanted to cash in on the title and actually had sixteen fights in the eleven months it took to make the match. The syndicate in charge at Manchester's Belle Vue arena where Brown was always a huge popular favourite finally came up with enough money to tempt Kirby into the decider in February 1931. The crowd of 7,000, mainly devoted Brown supporters, were given value for money by Jackie. He provided a perfect example of chanceless boxing, always first to the punch, slipping in and out constantly to do his scoring. He was totally unmarked, a clear points winner and champion again at the end, while little Bert's face was a contrasting map with bruises for mountains and blood for rivers.

They did, in fact, fight once more four years later when both had moved up to bantamweight - and by then Kirby, slower and battle scarred, was rescued by the referee in twelve rounds. Jackie Brown had gone on to much greater heights. He won the European title from a Rumanian, Lucien Popescu, in slightly farcical circumstances at Belle Vue in May 1931. Popescu came in overweight and refused to take off the extra poundage, but, after Brown had convincingly outpointed him, the existing rules enabled the Mancunian to claim the title and defend it successfully three times before the big one, a world title fight against Victor "Young" Perez, of Tunisia, again at Belle Vue in October 1932.

Little Jackie won the majority of his fights on points but perhaps because this fight was so special he found invaluable extra power after a fascinating and fluctuating twelve rounds. He dropped Perez in the thirteenth with the impeccable timing and accuracy of a left hook and a right cross to the head, then when the Tunisian got up, battered him so furiously that the towel came in and the fight was stopped. There was a tragic ending to the career of Perez. He was caught up in Nazi-occupied Europe where there was not much future for an undersized Arab and one line in the record book notes that he died in 1943 in Auschwitz.

Jackie Brown probably never realised how he was conned into taking on the most fearsome puncher ever in the flyweight division, Scotland's Benny Lynch, at Belle Vue in September 1935, in his fourth defence of the world title. Earlier the same year he had travelled to Glasgow to meet Lynch in a non-title fight and just before it started the mighty Scot received a set of instructions he could not at first believe from his canny manager, Sammy Wilson. "You'll need to hold back with him," said Wilson. "We don't want to give him a tanking or we'll no get a quick return for the title. Let him think he can beat you then we'll really sort him out." Every few rounds Benny would rebel and beg to be allowed to finish it. "Go easy with him Benny, easy", was always the answer. It was a draw.

The return took place and it was one of the most one-sided in championship history. With his first real punch, a left hook, Lynch knocked Brown down and kept on doing so every time he got up. There were five knock-downs in the first round. There were six in the second round and there was just about to be a seventh when Brown, dazed and in terrible pain from body punishment, appealed to the referee to stop the fight. There was obviously no longer any room in the flyweight division while Lynch was around, but Jackie Brown, still only 25, was far too good to be finished. He campaigned with reasonable success as a bantamweight, though his stablemate and champion in that division, Johnny King, beat him twice, including a thirteen-round knock-out with the title at stake in May 1937. Jackie still went on to complete a total of more than a hundred winning fights before retiring in 1939.

It was his left hand that did most of the work, but it is the right that Jackie Brown is proudly showing trainer Jack Bates.

Jackie Brown was brilliant boxing on retreat, so perhaps practising moving backwards on a rowing machine was useful.

PETER KANE
(1918 —   )

Produce a photograph of Peter Kane for anyone steeped in show business and they will unhesitatingly, and incorrectly, identify it instantly as the American singer-comedian of the thirties, Eddie Cantor. There is an uncanny resemblance in those huge dark soulful "banjo" eyes beneath thick, almost semi-circular brows, which create the impression of perpetual surprise. No one knows whether Eddie Cantor could fight, but no one doubts that Peter Kane certainly caused his own share of surprises. He came from Golborne, a Lancashire village halfway between Manchester and Liverpool, a place so insignificant that if you did not slow down travelling through you missed it. Peter Kane's name and fame put it on the map for ever.

Kane worked as an apprentice blacksmith, developing the muscle power that made him such a mighty hitter, and polished his boxing skills in the booths, before officially turning professional at sixteen, running up a stunning string of knock-outs. He had won 33 inside the distance and lost none of his first 41, most of them at Liverpool Stadium. It was the 41st that pushed him into the spotlight. He was matched against Ulsterman Jim Warnock in an official world title eliminator and, at nineteen, was distinctly second favourite. Warnock had twice beaten the reigning World Flyweight Champion, Benny Lynch, in overweight fights at a time when the only people who disputed whether Jimmy Wilde was the greatest flyweight of all time were those who insisted that Lynch was. It became a sensation when Kane swarmed all over the Irishman and knocked him out in four rounds.

That result quite literally sobered Benny Lynch for a while. He put the cork in the bottle that was to kill him tragically young at 33, went up into the Campsie Hills to train like a beast for six weeks for the fight in October 1937 at Shawfield Stadium, Glasgow, with 40,000 packed inside and thousands more locked out.

Maybe it was the inhibiting atmosphere for a lad more used to smaller halls, or maybe it was the respect he was entitled to show to a marvellous champion, but Kane did not make his usual whirlwind start. Impetuosity had always been his game, sustained aggression from the bell. Lynch, with the true instinct of a genuine fighting man, sensed the apprehension and with the first two real punches, left hook to the body, right cross to the chin – a classic one-two – had Kane into the ropes and down. Referee W. Barrington Dalby, a top official at the time and later the BBC Radio's resident inter-round summariser – "Come in Barrie" – had counted to only three before Kane was up again. It was far too soon but remember the young fighter had never previously been on the floor in his life. For him that had always been the other man's problem. Dalby, a tall man who towered over the two tiny warriors, was hardly seen and never noticed for another eleven rounds.

There were few clinches and those that occurred did not have to be broken up. Lynch and Kane had come to fight, not dance. Kane recovered so quickly from that first-round knock-down there were even ringside experts who gave him a share of the session's points. Certainly from then on the fight grew into universal recognition of its greatness in the whole history of world championship boxing. Two little men, each honed to superb fitness and masters of their craft, fought punch for punch. But it was never just a slugging match, there was too much craft and class for both to call upon. Both were always trying something, with Lynch even briefly adopting the southpaw style from which he had originally been converted.

One art of the game that Kane had not learned, however, was pacing a fight – maybe because he had never needed to. He had been taken to points only eight times in his career and this was his first fifteen-rounder. In the twelfth round Lynch planted his feet solidly for the leverage behind the best single punch of the hundreds thrown, a left hook smashed to Kane's head to drop him. Almost incredibly, certainly naïvely and providing further evidence of inexperience in what to do when hurt, he was up immediately. Pursued and punched all round the ring by an inflamed, exulting Lynch he was a helpless open target for a succession of left hooks. The partisan crowd which roared for their man were also applauding the astonishing resilience of Kane as he lurched to his corner. He rose from another inevitable knock-down at the start of the thirteenth at seven but, drained and dazed, another barrage put him down for the count. Barrington Dalby, who administered that count, always said Kane's was the bravest performance he had witnessed in his own long lifetime in the sport.

But the resilience in the frame and the spirit of young men like Kane has always had the recurring capability of astounding fight fans and six months later, less than a month after his twentieth birthday, Kane was

*Kane's best days were reckoned to be just memories when he came back
after the war. But that did not stop him decisively outpointing Theo Medina
to win a European Bantamweight title.*

matched against Lynch in a return. Again the Scot punished himself in training but, because he weighed in at a pound and a half over the limit for the bantamweight division, a class higher, the fight was reduced to a twelve-rounds non-title affair, ending in a draw. It was a good fight, but neither man had the incentive to produce another epic – and there was to be no third meeting, though Kane would have loved one.

Lynch, soaked in booze, forfeited the crown by failing yet again to make the weight against the American Jackie Jurich, who was instead nominated to meet Kane for the crown in September 1938. That was another unforgettable night for Peter Kane on his own ground at Anfield against a Californian who was highly rated as a speed merchant. The experts had overlooked how difficult it would become for any man to move at speed when the breath was regularly driven from his body by hooks to the ribs – always a spectacular Kane trade mark. Jurich was down a total of five times, three of them for counts of nine for an undisputed points victory by the Englishman. Kane, aged only twenty, was famous. The next ambition was to become rich – but, unhappily, the money-making years were lost to World War II. Kane joined up in the RAF and it was almost five years before he could defend his crown. Austerity, ring-rust, and an increasing difficulty in getting down to 8 stone all contributed to a one-round knock-out by Jackie Paterson.

Kane did not start a real comeback until 1946, when most reckoned that at 27 his best days were just an exciting memory. He was not given much of a chance of taking the European bantamweight title from a tough Frenchman, Theo Medina, who had stopped Kane's conqueror, Paterson, in four rounds, but that night in September 1947 Kane shrugged off the years. Medina was a squat, powerful, aggressive type who dominated the early rounds with work that was flashy and eye-catching – literally because he cut both Kane's brows – but it was noticeable that the initial storm left Kane unflustered. His impeccable footwork kept him out of bother and, gradually, superior and more correct punching started to count. He was clearly on top going into and through the last third of the fight.

Peter defended that title successfully against a Belgian, Joe Cornelius, but it could not last. The danger sign that the power and snap in his punches were diminishing arrived when he landed that famous left hook a dozen times to the head of a tough Italian challenger, Guido Ferracin, without any effect. He was outpointed easily and an attempt to regain it from the same man ended with defeat in five rounds, badly cut. There was only one more, a points defeat by Stan Rowan and when he retired at thirty in 1948 the irony was that he had never held a British title, but then he had never fought for one.

TERRY ALLEN
(1924 —   )

Terry Allen, the little cockney barrow boy from Islington, gave two young Scottish soldiers the treat of a lifetime when he made his final challenge for the World Flyweight title in Tokyo's Korakuen Stadium on 27 October 1953 against Yoshio Shirai of Japan. Private Eddie McArdle and Corporal Lewis Catley, two Royal Scots Fusiliers, were on the last night of leave from Korea in the Japanese capital at the time and were in no financial shape to buy ringside seats. It was typical of Terry Allen to make sure they had an even closer view than any of the 35,000 crammed into the arena. He engaged them as bucket holder and water carrier to work in his corner. But it was more than gratitude and patriotic prejudice which influenced and inflamed the two squaddies into a conviction that a fifteen-round points verdict which went against Allen was robbery.

Johnny Sharpe, Allen's manager throughout his career and a man who had his own claim to fame because he once beat Ted "Kid" Lewis when they were both flyweight tots, was furious. He felt that Terry had been up against two Japanese on the night, Shirai and a referee named Isamu. The official allowed Shirai to get away with slapping and never permitted the Londoner to sustain any two-fisted bursts to the body of the taller, skinnier Shirai - 5 feet 6 inches to Terry's 5 feet 2 inches. Whenever they came to close quarters he pulled Allen away forcibly. Although Allen set the pace for the first ten rounds he was virtually handcuffed, never able to do any slowing-down damage and an eye-catching rally in the last round after he had seemed to be fading through frustration did not impress the judges.

It had been a long, hard and disappointing journey to the other side of the world but then Terry Allen was always willing to travel anywhere, however hot and hostile, for a fight. He probably covered more miles - Honolulu and back twice, for instance - and boxed more fifteen-round championship fights than any post-war English boxer; nine of the eleven in his career went the distance.

He was born to the sort of background that soon convinces that the only thing money cannot buy is poverty – his mother died when he was a baby and he was brought up by his blind grandmother in the tough streets around Islington's Chapel Market where as a boy he humped potato sacks, hawked fruit and vegetables and eventually graduated to ownership of his own famous barrow. He was christened Edward "Teddy" Govier and started boxing under that name, winning more than a hundred amateur bouts before turning pro in 1942 with Johnny Sharpe, and within a few months joining the Royal Navy as, of all occupations for someone of his size, a stoker. Maybe that tough, hot job packed a tiny frame with even more strength because as Stoker Govier he won a string of wartime contests. He changed his name to Terry Allen as a tribute to the memory of a great friend and shipmate who was killed during the war.

Terry Allen was enormously popular with the Mediterranean Fleet, taking on a string of Egyptian bantamweights, flyweights and even occasional featherweights. Fifteen assorted Abduls, Hassans, Muhammads, Mustaphas and Sayids were defeated in succession before his demobilisation. The victories were achieved by bulldog aggression and determination – though he was built like a half-starved whippet.

Coming up even faster at the time was a gritty little Ulsterman, John Joseph Monaghan, who adopted the nickname Rinty out of affection for the Hollywood dog Rin-Tin-Tin. How Terry Allen ever passed the medical examination at the weigh-in for his first fight against Monaghan in April 1947 is not just a mystery, but a disgrace. Terry accepted the job as a last-minute substitute. He had just been released from hospital after a debilitating bout of malaria. It was no surprise he made the weight. He was a yellow-skinned bag of bones. Monaghan's first half-decent flurry of punches knocked him out in the first round. "If he'd only known," said a rueful Terry. "He could have blown me over." Why, then, did he take the fight? "I needed the money", was the reply.

It is one of the sad drawbacks of the flyweight division that, even though it has produced some murderously memorable little fighters and some epics of speed, skill and occasionally startling power, huge purses are rare. That is probably mainly because in America, land of the really big money, the attitude to flyweights usually veers between lukewarm interest and slight contempt. Tex Rickard, probably that nation's slickest promoter, once summed it up with wry, sly humour: "Guys as small as that shouldn't come to blows. They should go see their lawyers."

Allen was obsessed by that Monaghan defeat, only his second in 40 fights. He continually pestered his manager to "Get me that Rinty again". It took almost two years and it was an overweight match that was signed because by then Monaghan was champion of the world, after knocking out in six rounds the great Scot Jackie Paterson – or rather what was left of a boiled down and burnt out Paterson.

Terry Allen was probably at his brilliant best that February night in 1949. Scintillating boxing at high speed won him every round and, although he was never a big puncher, he actually had Monaghan down. Terry Allen felt absolutely certain that over the championship distance he would knock out the Irishman. He was wrong. When they met in Belfast's King's Hall the following September little Rinty, although already suffering from the tuberculosis that caused his retirement after that fight, put it all together one more time. Although Allen had him down in the second round no one quarrelled when the fight was scored a draw, and Monaghan went out of the game as champion. It was in truth a rather disappointing fight, perhaps because similar styles and a healthy mutual respect cancelled each other out.

With the title vacant, Allen had to wait only two more fights to become World Flyweight Champion – on 25 April 1950 after fifteen rounds against Honore Pratesi, a muscular brawling Frenchman who had clearly outpointed him a year earlier and was strongly fancied to do the same again. Allen shook everyone, particularly Pratesi, not merely by comprehensively outboxing him at long range – that was to be expected – but by punching it out eagerly at the toe to toe game also. As well as the lifetime target of the world title there was the bonus of a European crown too – even though it did not last. He went to Honolulu to lose the

Rinty Monaghan, Flyweight Champion of the world, crouches to avoid Allen's jabs, but the Londoner still won a ten-rounds points decision.

world crown on a narrow points verdict to Dado Marino, the 34-year-old Hawaian who became the first grandfather ever to take the title, and was more controversially outpointed on his return by the talented Belgian, Jean Sneyers, who took his European title.

Still, the British title was vacant and a clear points win by the still talented Terry over Vic Herman, a colourful and tough little Scottish boxer, was preceded by one of the most hideous rows ever experienced at a ringside. Herman used to play himself into the ring blowing bagpipes, so the mischievous Allen insisted on being accompanied by a piano accordian playing cockney songs. In the awful cacophony it was impossible to spot the tune. Nominating the winner was easy, however – even though Allen was knocked down by the last punch of the fight.

The end of the glory days was in sight. A return trip to Honolulu saw Grandpa Marino, improving with age, punish as well as outpoint him. The Shirai fight in Tokyo came between Allen regaining and retaining his British title against a Northerner, Eric Marsden – and ominously that second victory came when Marsden, well in front at the time, was disqualified for a sixth-round low punch. There was one more title fight, another points defeat in Italy by Nazzareno Gianelli. It was Terry's last fight, but the real warning sign came in the last but one. It had always taken a considerable puncher to do Terry Allen any damage, but the up and coming Welsh lad who stopped him in two rounds, Dai Dower, was always reckoned a powder-puff puncher who could not break an egg even wearing knuckle dusters.

Eric Marsden is stopped in the sixth round with Terry regaining his British Flyweight title.

CHARLIE MAGRI
(1 9 5 6 —   )

Charlie Magri created one record that seems likely to remain intact for many years. When he challenged for the British Flyweight title in December 1977, aged 21, his whole professional career could be measured in minutes rather than fights or even rounds. He had had only about ten minutes of actual combat, two victories inside two rounds. The Board of Control were even a mite anxious about sanctioning as a championship a fight with Dave Smith. They should have been more worried about Smith. One of the four knock-downs he suffered in a defeat inside seven rounds sent him somersaulting through the ropes on to a press typewriter.

Charlie was, of course, even then, a fairly seasoned fighter, winner of four ABA titles, a stocky, compact, well-muscled little man, very fast and a quick mover and puncher. He was managed from the start by that promoter's nightmare, Terry Lawless, a man so protective of his "family" of boxers that he traces the pedigree of every suggested opponent carefully and anxiously. In the terse, colourful language of his trade he "just don't wanna know" when anyone too potentially dangerous is put forward. His attitude about his new champion in the early days was, "He is an excellent prospect, that's all. He might become a European championship contender, but not yet. And you are not going to see me pitch him in against any of those tough Mexican monkeys for a while." Magri was fed a steady diet of not-too-menacing men, knocking them all over or busting them up badly. Only one of his first eleven opponents went the distance. The rest lasted an average of less than three rounds. Twice during Charlie's first two years as professional, Lawless turned down invitations for him to box for the European title. When asked what made him finally accept a crack at a very tough veteran, Franco Udella, a 32-year-old former World Champion who had held the title for five years, Lawless said, "Because it is time. I've tried really hard to provide him with opponents who can extend him and Charlie has just turned them over, destroyed them."

Charlie learned a lot against Udella, one of the very few opponents shorter than himself, on that May night in 1979. Perhaps the most important was that at the higher levels there were men who could take his best shots, not merely without wilting but without stepping back. Still, one man who had no doubt about the verdict was Udella. Without waiting for the announcement he hoisted Magri's hand, embraced and applauded him. "He is the best I ever met and no, I don't want a return. I don't want to go through that again," said the Italian.

By the time of his first defence, Magri was looking a complete craftsman, winning just about every round against the only other opponent who had so far lasted the distance with him, Spanish champion Manuel Carrasco. For him it became the night of a thousand punches, all of them landing on him – jabs, hooks, crosses, uppercuts. Magri was undefeated in 1980 and growing steadily in public esteem to warrant top of the bill status in major promotions at Wembley. He built a string of 23 winning fights, only four of which went the distance. Three were against men who had won world titles – Udella, Santos Laciar of

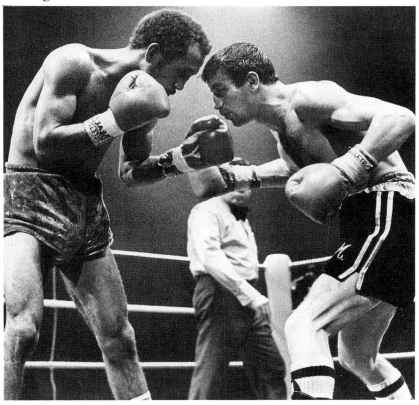

Magri crouches into menacing action as he sets about winning the world title from Eloncio Mercedes at Wembley.

187

Argentina, and Alfonso Lopez of Panama. Carrasco was a former European champion.

Magri was steaming steadily, smoothly, it seemed inexorably, in the direction of the world title, when that idea had to be put on the back burner. His reputation started to suffer from an accusation he bitterly resented and disputed to the end of his career – a claim that he suffered the most disastrous defect in a fighter, a glass jaw. It started in a fairly meaningless keep-the-pot-boiling fight against a Mexican, Juan Diaz, at the Albert Hall. Charlie boxed rings round him for five rounds, then walked face first into a hard right, was dropped and stopped. "The geezer hit me with a good shot when I lost concentration for a second. It could happen to anyone. It has happened to hundreds of fighters," he maintained.

The snag was it happened twice more to Charlie against Mexicans in 1982. It began to look to some critics as though Charlie was like a punter who had the right eight crosses on a treble chance football pools coupon and then got knocked down by a bus on his way to post it. The gods gave him almost everything it takes to be the best and then withheld durability. Although Magri outpointed the first of those Mexicans, Cipriano Arreola, he was knocked down at the end of the ninth and had to hang on grimly to survive the tenth. The second one, José Torres, stopped him in nine rounds – and although Charlie won a brave and brilliant return, he was again hurt in the final round. Still, that took him to where he had always wanted to be, though the road was rather longer than it might have been – to the Wembley ring in March 1983, facing Eloncio Mercedes of the Dominican Republic, Flyweight Champion of the world. Almost magically it all came flowing back to Magri. He showed resilience in taking the best shots Mercedes threw, long looping rights to the head. He showed intelligence in concentrating his attacks in the early rounds to the body, bringing the guard down and the head in range. It created the opportunity to cut his man in the sixth and pound away so accurately that the fight had to be stopped in the seventh.

Charlie Magri was on top of the world, but staying there is sometimes harder than getting there. In his first defence he boxed brilliantly to establish a clear points lead over Filipino Frank Cedeno for five rounds. Then the vulnerability he still stubbornly denies, saw him caught, hurt and down three times before it was stopped in the sixth.

He was to get one more world championship chance seventeen months later when the world by then had a far better and stronger champion than it had known for some time. Charlie was in it for only a brief spell, then the quicker, tougher and even harder-hitting Sot Chitalada of Thailand cut and battered him severely. His corner

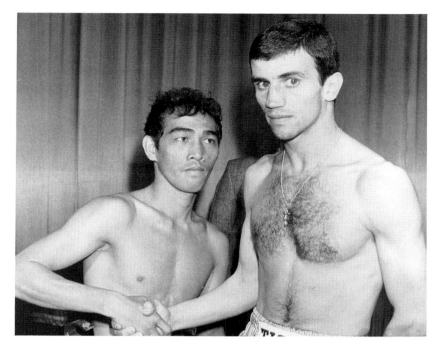

There seems some apprehension on Magri's face, a threatening look about
Cedeno at their weigh-in. Both were justified. Cedeno won in six.

mercifully retired him. There was no longer any room at the top for
Charlie Magri and it was the only place he wanted to be. He became one
of the best-loved boxers of them all, a genuine charmer outside the ring,
so naturally nice and mild and friendly that the first reaction he inspired
in most people was to give him a cuddle. Opponents who had been
ripped from a clinch by his startling physical strength and then stunned
by the ferocity of his hooking would advise against it. The only thing
guaranteed to rile him was to knock boxing. Without it he reckons he
would have been just another member of life's anonymous work-force –
his first paid job was as an assistant milk roundsman to Johnny Robinson,
who is still one of his close friends. By the time he retired he owned his
house and a sports goods business. The name and title above the shop do
no harm at all to the trade.

   The only visible sign of that trade is a nose that has been
comprehensively flattened and distorted by punches. He did toy with
the idea of having it corrected with plastic surgery until his wife Jackie
threatened that if he did she would rearrange it the very next day in the
same old shape. She likes him the way he is – and that goes for all of those
privileged to know him.

Page numbers in **bold** type refer to major sections, including pictures. Other illustrations are indicated by *italic* type.

Photographic Acknowledgements
Boxing News
13, 15, 81, 83, 100 (below), 102, 127, 128, 140 (below), 149, 157, 163, 165. *Brian Tarleton Private Collection* 150, 151, 152. *Hulton Picture Library* 17, 19, 26, 27, 47 (below), 48, 49, 50, 51, 53, 54, 68, 71, 76, 97, 100 (above), 104, 132, 136, 140 (above), 141, 169, 184, 185. *Keystone Picture Library* 22, 23, 30, 31, 32, 33, 37, 47 (above), 57, 63, 79 (below), 109, 114, 115, 134, 139, 142, 145, 171, 177, 187. *Sport and General* 90, 93, 95, 96, 155. *Syndication International* 35, 38, 39, 41, 43, 44, 45, 61, 62, 119, 121. *Topham Picture Library* 25, 36, 58, 64, 73, 75, 77, 79 (below), 85, 87, 99, 107, 110, 118, 124, 147, 161, 173, 180, 189.